I0145083

DEAD FLIES

Steven Grant Burgess

Published by Snowflake Publishing, 625 Cass Avenue, Moore, Oklahoma, 73160

ISBN 978-0-9821798-2-6

Printed in the United States of America

For further information inquires may be sent to bburgessgrant@sbcglobal.net

Other publications by the author-The Chronicle of Tnarg

INTRODUCTION

If you have picked up this book thinking it might be a tome of literary genius and acumen, you are going to be sadly disappointed. In many ways it is quite ordinary and in some parts may leave the reader wondering why the topic wasn't further clarified. But that aside, hopefully it may edify some, cause reflection for others, and primarily be a means by which the gospel of Jesus Christ is proclaimed to those who never heard this good news, or need to hear it again.

Except for three or four of the chapters, this is a small compilation of articles, if you can even call them articles, written over the last twenty years, and as you will see, many of the articles have some sort of reference back to the gospel. Though they were written for the Christian disciple, it was hoped that many unbelievers would read them as well. As it turned out, very few people (as far as we know) ever read them.

What started out as a website called the Christian Disciple was soon changed to a blog of the same name. There were a handful of readers, and it was decided many more would be reached on Facebook, which will now and then be referenced by FB. How many actually read anything is something we have no way of knowing. However, whether positive or negative, there were only a handful of responses. The response that really mattered is the one that came just before Covid really took off in March of 2020. It was then that FB closed out my account for what it deemed as violating community standards. It wasn't a suspension, but a permanent deleting of the account. As an aside, in 2025 when President Trump took office, FB changed their policies. I was able to open up a new account using my first name, but it is being used solely for Marketplace, not for the writing of articles. E-mail was another option, but it seemed like an invasion of people's privacy, so after two or three articles we just quit.

When FB did close my account in 2020, almost everything that was written was lost. Changing computers a few years earlier had caused others to be lost, but not all of them. Some of the ones that had been written on the blog were able to be retrieved, and a handful of those from FB had been written, copied and pasted, so not all was lost. Recently, while looking over what had been saved, and realizing in some areas that I had regressed in my Christian walk, I decided to compile a group of them for me to review from time to time.

As a Christian, nothing we have is truly our own, and as we have opportunity, we are to share with others. This is just a feeble attempt to do that. Again, many of these articles were written with the unbeliever in mind, so there may be many that find it very elementary, especially when it comes to some of the theological ones. In a two or three page article it is difficult if not impossible to articulate an idea that in most books have several pages devoted to the introduction. But hopefully the appetite will be whetted enough to cause the reader to pursue a greater understanding of that particular area of theology. If so, we should hope to see a domino effect. We study parts of a whole, and we cannot truly know one part without seeing how it relates to other parts in this system. And so we have systematic theology.

This is my primary field of study, along with the bible, and at times it can be quite distressing to see the lack of doctrinal understanding among those who have been Christians for many years. What it says in Hebrews 5 about those who are dull of hearing is most likely appropriate in every generation. If we are dull in hearing we will constantly be learning basic principles of Christianity, always needing milk, not solid food. We remain children as it were and never mature; this should not be. At the same time, it must be biblical doctrine, not just denominational doctrine. It is true that there are a handful of secondary issues that denominations disagree on, but it is secondary, and not crucial. All Christian denominations agree that there is no possibility of salvation without faith in Jesus Christ. But some believe that God is Sovereign in salvation, and some believe it is a work of man. Those who believe that it is a work of man might word it differently. They might say a man chooses to believe or not, but no one comes to Jesus unless he is drawn by the Father. Let's leave that for now, but you get the point.

But doctrine doesn't just fall into our lap. It must primarily be learned through the reading and preaching of the word of God, and for most people it will come through the preaching. But if our preachers and teachers don't have a love or knowledge of theology, it will not get passed on to the hearer. If they have been to seminary, then they almost certainly had a class or two in theology, but for many of them it was a required course, and they just did the work so they could get on to graduation. It was a means to an end, so they could enter the ministry. But we have to ask, why did they enter the ministry if not to proclaim the full word of God? How can you proclaim the full word of God if you don't have a proficient understanding and love for it all?

The greatest ministers seem to be those who have an unquenchable desire to increase in their love and knowledge of God, and to instill that same desire into their listeners. It was my original aim years ago to teach theology at a seminary level and perhaps have a part in instilling that love for the knowledge of God into others. But by making a couple of wrong choices and being naïve, I thought learning the material would be enough, and never got a degree. Like I said, I was naïve, but the desire for others to know God has never gone away, just squashed. This was the original aim in writing these small articles; to make the knowledge of God grow in the reader, and to encourage them in their Christian walk, while at the same time perhaps proclaiming the gospel to unbelievers. Whether or not that occurred is hard to tell, and whether or not this avenue will be fruitful is equally unknown.

If you are curious as to why we named the book Dead Flies, it is because several years ago I wrote an article called Dead Flies which was posted to a blog I had at the time. It generated more traffic than any other article, which I had written, so it was reposted a year or so ago, and got a similar response.

Admittedly, it was probably the title that drew attention, but sometimes that is what it takes to get someone interested in what you have to say.

Except for some minor editing these short notes are what we sent out in the past, and are not always weighty in thought, but we hope you like them. Again, my apologies to any of you who think this is poorly written, and was just thrown together, to a certain extent you are right. Further editing was not my intention when putting this all together, and while there is that concern that no one will be interested in future writings, ultimately it is the glory of God we are interested in proclaiming, not our own or the readers.

As I always do when ending a post, I bid you Shalom.

DEAD FLIES

Dead flies cause the ointment of the apothecary to send forth a stinking savour: so doth a little folly him that is in reputation for wisdom and honor.

What we will be looking at and dissecting, or if you prefer expositing, is a simple verse from the book of Ecclesiastes, which is found in the Bible, the Word of God. It is hard sometimes not to go off on a tangent here, but when we speak of the Word of God, the Bible, we are speaking of the revelation which God has given to mankind. It is the truth without variance, and we are wise to treat it as such. That unregenerate men hold the truth to be irrelevant is not our topic here, but simply one simple verse encompassed among thousands of others. Yet each is a statement from God to be used by mankind for his edification, or for another instance of his condemnation. This gets into much doctrine and theology which distracts from our verse, so let us move on.

It is our intent as we unravel this verse to encourage ourselves, exhort ourselves and to remember what a mighty God we serve. Of course if you are serving God and glorifying God, we assume you are a Christian, and we are writing from that perspective. Yet, in the back of our mind, we realize that the vast majority of people in this world are lost, and are serving God and glorifying God in a negative sense. We have only to look at the book of Romans to see this clearly illustrated.

But we are writing this short expose to Christians as an encouragement, and an exhortation. However, this verse has universal application, by which is meant that its truth can be attested to by those who never darken the door of a church as well as the regenerate. It is timeless as well, and although some of the wording may need explaining, those who hear it today understand it just as well as those who first heard it three thousand years ago.

There is a most interesting saying in Ecclesiastes about dead flies and in the old English of the King James Version of the bible it says that dead flies cause the ointment of the apothecary to send forth a stinking savour. This is just a fancy way of saying that dead flies cause the perfumers ointment to stink. It doesn't seem possible that just a couple of flies could cause such a stink, but I have dealt with tiny ghost shrimp that are only about an inch long, and when they die, they can cause a whole room to stink. Just one can cause a room to smell like fecal matter, so a can see where a couple of dead flies can cause ointment to stink.

But the proverb goes on to say that just as these flies cause the ointment to stink, so does a little folly to a man renowned for wisdom and honor. Folly, that momentary lack of sense, or bad behavior, can ruin a lifetime of right living, and we see it happen all the time. In fact, you can look at the news of today and see a man who everyone thought was good, but now has been accused of sexual misconduct. (This was originally written in 2010) Now it still remains to be seen if these accusations are in fact true, but we all know of someone who we respected that fell into disrepute for a momentary lack of discretion. Just recently, 2024, there was a nationally known preacher and teacher whom this happened to, and it should sadden us all. But it happens to ordinary Christians as well, and while we may never know them, somebody does. A moment of folly can and usually ruins a lifetime of good reputation. If you look at many of the words that are similar to folly, it describes the act very well. It is a stupid act lacking foresight, and while sin is not one of the definitions, most often sin is involved.

Such is the character of sin; it is a stupid act lacking foresight. We tend to view sin as those big things, such as murder, stealing, etc., and measure our own shortcomings as insignificant, because they are just little white lies, or we just borrowed that pencil from work and never brought it back. It is those little things that we ignore, because they seem so petty. Think for a few minutes on those things that you might allow yourself to do that if people found out they would doubt your Christianity? It could be something like going out to the casino or perhaps the club to meet up with the guys after work. We need to think on this, because we are on display before the world, and they are just looking for something to accuse us of. Generally, folly is much more than this, but what does God think?

God says that the soul which sins shall die. There isn't really any wiggle room for discussion, and all sin is a stench to His nostrils. It is because they are so small, like dead flies and ghost shrimp, that we think they are insignificant, but to God, they cause a stinking savour. We think we are okay with God because we compare ourselves to others, but fail to remember that He demands perfection.

It can't be done by us, but the whole point of the gospel, is that Jesus has done everything necessary for our salvation in order to satisfy the wrath of God against our sin. We only have to repent (turn to God and away from our sin) and believe in Christ. Sounds simple enough, but will YOU believe? Your decision will have eternal consequences. Until we meet again, Shalom.

TELL EM WHO YOU ARE

I had an interesting dream last night that I would like to share as it may be informative to all of us. Dreams serve many purposes, but one purpose is to educate us in some form or another. Now whether this is the Holy Spirit, our conscience, or a figment of our imagination teaching us, the reader can decide. Since I don't know either, I will just call it a teachable moment and leave it at that.

It all started in one of those old run down missions such as you used to see in some of the bigger downtown cities, which I suppose may still be around. It was a small building, but was pretty much filled to capacity with the type of patrons you would expect, winos with a few homeless people and a few of the women who worked the streets getting in from the cold. Apparently a popular preacher was going to be speaking that night and couldn't make it. There was another preacher there, quite elderly, and he had brought his grandson who was learning to be a preacher to hear this other preacher speak. When the people who ran the mission found out that there was another preacher there, they asked if he would speak for them a few minutes, but being elderly and somewhat feeble he declined while informing them that his grandson would be capable. Of course the grandson was caught off guard, but not wanting to disappoint, said he would, but then turned to his grandfather and asked what he should speak about.

At first (in the dream anyway) it seemed kind of lame, but the grandfather just looked at him and said "Son, just tell em who you are." And that is exactly what he did. Of course he told them his name, where he lived and was going to school, and then threw in a few other details about his life and that was it. It lasted about ten minutes and then it was all over. Everyone milled about talking for a little while, and then the dream transferred into another scene completely different.

It was at night, and several of us were traveling in one of those old convertible roadsters that had running boards that you could stand on. I didn't really know anyone there, and there were three of us standing on each running board, and there were six or seven people seated in the car. (Remember this is a dream, so don't go writing me that this isn't possible) I don't remember for sure where we were going, except that it was to a place that we shouldn't have been going to. It seems as if we were going to one of those out of the way houses out in the country where gambling and drinking and loose women were on the menu. It was right out of one of those b-rated movies you might see at some run down drive-in. Anyway, I looked down at the passengers and to my surprise, the young man who had spoken at the mission was sitting there and some woman was wrapped all around him waiting for a more opportune time to continue carousing in private. I won't say what I heard being said, but it goes without saying, it wasn't wholesome.

We came to a stop, and I grabbed him by the collar, yanked him out of the car, which proceeded to drive off, and berated him, asking him, don't you know who you are? You are a child of the King, the Lord and Creator of the universe, you have been saved to eternal life by the precious sacrifice of Jesus, you are an ambassador for Christ, educating yourself in how to speak and proclaim the gospel on His behalf, and you're behaving like this? You have been saved from your sin and the wrath of God, and been translated from a kingdom of darkness into one of light, and this is the thanks you return? This is what your grandpa meant when he told you to tell them who you are, and then I woke up.

I can't tell you what this all means for sure, and of course it might mean different things to different people, but one thing is clear, and that is that when it is necessary, tell them who you are. One of the major ways in which we do this, is by our actions, what we say, what we do, and where we go, and by how we spend our time. So how is that going for you? Are you going or doing or seeing anything which might not be in step with who you are? It might not be anything drastic like it was in the dream, but see if it applies, and if not that is a good thing.

"And if you call on him as Father who judges impartially according to each one's deeds, conduct yourselves with fear throughout the time of your exile, knowing that you were ransomed from the futile ways inherited from your forefathers, not with perishable things such as silver or gold, but with the precious blood of Christ, like that of a lamb without blemish or spot." 1 Peter 1:17-19 (ESV)

Think on these things, and until next time, Shalom.

THE CHRISTIAN DISCIPLE

"Will we continue to march to the drumbeat of conformity and respectability, or will we listen to the beat of a more distant drum? Will we move to its echoing sounds? Will we march only to the music of time, or will we, risking criticism and abuse, March to the soul saving music of eternity? More than ever before, we are today challenged by the words of yesterday, 'Be not conformed to this world, but be transformed by the renewing of your mind' "-Martin Luther King Jr.

"I beseech you therefore, brethren, by the mercies of God, that you present your bodies a living sacrifice, holy, acceptable to God, which is your reasonable service. And do not be conformed to this world, but be transformed by the renewing of your mind, that you may prove what is that good and acceptable and perfect will of God."- Romans 12:1-2

We are the Disciples of Christ. When we tell people who we are, shouldn't that really be the first thing that comes to mind? Invariably when we meet someone for the first time, the question is asked, "What do you do?" How often do you reply, "I follow Christ." We know to a large extent that someone's identity is tied to their occupation, but shouldn't the Christian's main occupation be following Christ?

Quite a few years ago we started out trying to have a website, then moved to a blog, neither of which was very successful, and then moved to FB until we were banned off of there. They were all called the Christian Disciple, for that is what the Christian is, a disciple of Christ. We are learners, hopefully becoming more and more like our teacher and Lord, Jesus Christ. But at the same time we need to be aware of the difference between learning what Jesus taught, and living what Jesus taught. A Christian is a disciple of Christ, living out what He taught, though we do so imperfectly, being empowered by the Holy Spirit dwelling in us, to greater and greater degrees of sanctification. We stumble often, many times grieving and quenching that Spirit that dwells within us, letting that person we used to be get the upper hand.

A Christian is a new creation, we have been born again as it were, and we are automatically disciples, or we are not really Christians. That sounds a little harsh because we forget that we are all at different levels of maturity. Someone who has just become a Christian may be completely unaware of those activities and behaviors we should no longer practice. Those real struggles are when we do know what to refrain from, but want to do it anyway. Sometimes we are the bug, sometimes the windshield, yet we continue to follow our Lord desiring to be obedient. If you do not have that desire to be obedient, then why would you call yourself a Christian? Did you not count the cost?

In the gospels we have the story of the rich young ruler who came to Jesus one day and asked what he must do to inherit eternal life? After Jesus names off several of the commandments, this young man says he has kept all these from his youth. And I want us to especially look at what is written in Mark 10:21-"And Jesus, looking at him, loved him," we will look at the rest of the verse in a minute, but what was it about this young man that Jesus loved? Then I look in the mirror and think, why did or why would Jesus love me? But then I remember that verse, "By Grace you have been saved"; Jesus loves me this I know, for the bible tells me so. Jesus goes on to say to this man, "You lack one thing: go, sell all that you have and give to the poor, and you will have treasure in heaven; and come, follow me." (ESV)

"Come, follow me." Isn't that what Jesus has said to each and every one of us? You can't DO anything to inherit eternal life, just follow Jesus. The first few verses of Isaiah 55 remind us of the same thing, return to God, come, follow me. But this rich young ruler had great possessions, and went away sorrowfully. The things of this world were more important to him than eternal life. We read of others in the bible who valued their life in this world more important than their eternal destiny in the next, but we also read of those who went about in the skins of sheep and goats, who were destitute, afflicted, and mistreated, and the world was not worthy of them. It just reminds us to think about that person living on the streets, homeless, and barely getting by. They might just be one of our brothers and sisters in Christ whom we will spend eternity with in heaven. Regardless, they have also been made in the image of God, so it behooves us to think a little more kindly of them then we usually do. Look at Moses, who chose to be mistreated with the people of God, and considered the reproach of Christ greater wealth than the treasures of Egypt. He considered the reward of so much greater value; eternal life with God.

There was a day when the crowds were following Jesus, and turning to them he said that unless they hated their family, (meaning caring for Him more than for them) even their own life they couldn't be his disciples. Not only that, but to take up their own cross, renounce all that they had, and if not, they couldn't be his disciple. The call to follow Christ for eternal life hasn't changed, but neither has the cost. But in today's modern world, and in reality, even back then, we want to have God on our own terms, we want what Dietrich Bonhoeffer called cheap grace, a grace without a cost.

It is a grace we acquire by faith, but we will only have it on our terms, not on the terms God requires. Now we all agree that faith, not our works, is necessary for salvation, but we would all probably also agree that faith without works, which is the fruit of the Holy Spirit indwelling each believer, is dead. If there is no evidence of salvation then there is great need of soul searching. We would have Christ on our terms, but not His. It is easy enough to attend church regularly, read our bibles and pray, all of which are good and necessary things and not to be downgraded in importance. But each one of you knows in your heart that Jesus has asked more of you. In fact, if you are a Christian, something unique has happened to you, and that is that you have died. Galatians 2:20 is not the only verse we could look at, but spend some time truly meditating on what that means. We have died to this world's ways, and have been as it says in Colossians 1:13, translated into the Kingdom of God's dear Son. We are now citizens of heaven, not earth, though we pilgrimage down here. Now what does this look like, or what are the ramifications? It means we will be obedient to the commands of Christ, or in rebellion, in which case be prepared for chastisement.

We must take up our cross and die, and as Bonhoeffer said, "We have forgotten that the cross means rejection and shame as well as suffering." This is not natural in our fallen state, which is why we struggle with it so much. The natural man says I want salvation, but it must be a life of ease. The natural man says I want salvation, but only if I can retain my pride. The natural man says I want salvation, but the world must love me. Fire insurance is what the natural man wants, but to be a disciple of Christ requires obedience, and he will have none of it.

But true Christians struggle with obedience as well, and God deals with them as He sees fit. Once we see ourselves as truly dead, obedience becomes much easier. Once we see ourselves as dead to sin, but alive to righteousness, it also becomes easier. And if we can see ourselves as slaves, bought not with a price of gold and silver, but with the atoning blood of Christ shed on our behalf; we are not our own, it becomes easier.

We are in fact slaves, bondservants, and our time is not our own, our talents and abilities are not our own, and our treasure is not our own. All of it has been given to us to use, not necessarily for our own benefit, but as a steward in the household of God. We need to get to that point in our life where we can say or ask, is my time being used in a way that demonstrates stewardship or ownership? Do you really think time is a possession you can use as you will? The same goes with the abilities God has given us. Some come naturally, and some are attained, but they are all from the hand of God, and are you using them in a proper manner? Then the hardest of all, our treasure. Do you really think it is yours? We say we honor God by giving Him a portion on a regular basis, but if we give 10 percent and claim possession over the other 90 percent, we may be in for a rude awakening. There is no need to go into this at this time, but is your treasure being spent on frivolities of this life to please yourself rather than God? Only you can answer that.

Realize that as I write this, I struggle with this as much as the next person, and there is not a cookie cutter answer I can give. Perhaps you are a golfer with some ability, and some or much of your time and money is spent playing this game. It is not for me to say how you spend your time and money, for this may be one of those pleasures in life that God has given you to enjoy. But, have you thought about it? Maybe you are one of those parents who spends an enormous amount of time and money on sporting events in which your children participate. Do they take precedent over God? Each one of us has things like this in our life which we need to meditate on and ask God if we need to make adjustments.

When the answer comes, then obedience is required, but we must begin to ask ourselves these questions if we would be Disciples of Christ. There is no option besides obedience if you are a Christian. There will be struggle and failure at times, or at least I have found it to be so in my life, but we have that great promise that confession and repentance bring cleansing.

In closing, I will leave you with a few tidbits from the life of C.T. Studd. Listen to what he said on more than one occasion. "If Jesus Christ is God and died for me, then no sacrifice can be too great for me to make for Him."

Now it is said that an article written by an atheist was what spurred Mr. Studd to all out dedication to Christ. As you consider your time, talents and treasure, see if this article by an atheist does not only convict you, but spur you on to greater discipleship and work for the Kingdom of God. I could not find who this atheist was that wrote this but take it to heart.

"If I firmly believed, as millions say they do, that the knowledge and practice of religion in this life influences destiny in another, then religion would mean to me everything. I would cast away earthly enjoyments as dross, earthly cares as follies, and earthly thoughts and feelings as vanity. Religion would be my first waking thought and my last image before sleep sank me into unconsciousness. I should labor in its cause alone. I would take thought for the morrow of Eternity alone. I would esteem one soul gained for heaven worth a life of suffering. Earthy consequences would never stay my hand, or seal my lips. Earth, its joys and its griefs, would occupy no moments of my thoughts. I would strive to look upon Eternity alone, and on the immortal souls around me, soon to be everlastingly happy or everlastingly miserable. I would go forth to the world and preach to it in season and out of season, and my text would be, WHAT SHALL IT PROFIT A MAN IF HE GAIN THE WHOLE WORLD AND LOSE HIS OWN SOUL?"

Tell em who you are. Shalom.

KNOWING GOD?

When writing or speaking to an audience that is primarily composed of Christians, it is easy to overlook those who are not. We previously looked at how a little foolish act can destroy a reputation, and that happens among unbelievers just as well as believers, so they understand. But when it comes to sin, especially what we erroneously call little sins, it becomes a little different. After all, is taking a pencil home from work really that big of deal? Or what about breaking the speed limit, is that such a big deal? To the unbeliever, as well as to many believers it isn't, but again, we must ask ourselves the more important question, what does God say about it?

Admittedly, God has never said anything about pencils or speed limits, but He has let us know His mind when it comes to stealing and obeying governments. And before we move on, there is something we need to consider and apply. In the Garden of Eden, Adam and Eve were at liberty to eat of all the fruits of the tree except one. They had the freedom to indulge and delight in everything that God had given them, but they weren't to eat of the fruit from the tree of the knowledge of good and evil. So much freedom, yet they somehow thought that God was restricting them, holding them back, keeping them from something that would make their life better.

But didn't God clearly warn them what would happen if they ate from the tree? That in the day that they ate from it they would die? Wasn't He protecting them from harm, doing it for their own good? Parents warn their children about dangers all the time. Not that they are trying to restrict them, but to protect them from harm. There is more involved in this event, because it also includes obedience. To simplify it, we punish our children in some way or another for disobeying us, and likewise, God punished Adam and Eve for disobeying Him, and that punishment was death.

Now we look at that and say or think, what is the big deal? All they did was eat a piece of fruit; it was a momentary lack of judgement, a dead fly. The BIG deal is that they did not believe God. Unfortunately, we do that all the time. But before we get further involved in this, we need to get back to that unbeliever.

Should we define what we mean by unbeliever? It simply means that they do not believe that Jesus of Nazareth is the Christ, the Son of God, fully God as well as fully human, and lived a perfect sinless life, died on the cross, was buried, and arose from the dead three days later, ascended to heaven , and will return to judge mankind. And also, in believing that he died for their sins, asking for forgiveness and asking to be saved; having faith that he can do so. We include in this category those who have never heard these truths, for if they have not heard, then they cannot believe.

There is a passage in Romans 10 that deals with this, and it says that everyone who calls upon the name of the Lord shall be saved. But it goes on to say or ask, how can they call on him whom they have not believed, and how are they to believe in someone they have never heard of, and how are they to hear unless someone declares or preaches it to them? "Faith comes by hearing, and hearing by the word of God." It is necessary that this was mentioned, because it is only by faith in Christ, that a man or women or child can be saved.

This naturally raises a few more questions, the most important one being, saved from what? Also, how can someone be held responsible for believing in something or someone which they have never heard about? And lastly, for now, how can we know if any of this is true? These are honest questions which deserve honest answers, and while this book is more of a collection of past articles, it does answer them, though not necessarily in an exhaustive way. But we have tried to arrange these articles in as orderly a way as we could. Likewise, we have just put some in which stand alone.

We have strayed a little from this chapter head, "Knowing God?" in order to bring up a few topics that without knowing God wouldn't make sense. At the same time, if you don't know who God is, not only does it not make sense, but you could care less. It goes back to our Romans 10 passage; it is necessary to hear.

It is necessary for us to regress a little bit and ask, if it is possible to know God, how is that going to happen? After all, the questions we asked earlier can only be answered after we have an understanding of who God is. And the only way we can understand or know who God is, is if He gives us a revelation of Himself. So it is possible to know God, but only so far as He reveals Himself to mankind and that revelation is in the Word of God which we call the Bible.

So the next time we meet, we will spend a little time on the topic of the Bible, because it is our only foundation for the truths of God and the knowledge of God and why it matters. Until then, Shalom.

THE WORD OF GOD

All scripture is breathed out by God and profitable for teaching, for reproof, for correction, and for training in righteousness, (2 Timothy 3:16 (ESV)

The last time we met it was mentioned that the only way we could know God was if He revealed Himself to us, and that He had done so in what we call the Bible. Now to the Christian reading this, it is one of those "DUH" moments; but not so quick. Unfortunately there are those who profess to be Christians that do not consider the Bible to be the ultimate authority for their lives, but hopefully by time we finish, they will realize what an oxymoron it is to call themselves a Christian and not to hold to the truths of their Creator. Part, if not most of the problem lies in the fact that over the last couple of centuries, more intellectual effort has been given to disprove the authority of the bible as a standard of truth. This is done in a variety of ways, but usually in one form or another by discrediting those essential doctrines of Christianity. One example might be the virgin birth of Jesus. If they can prove, which they can't, that Jesus was just an ordinary individual like the rest of us, then other doctrines fall with it. While it is not our intention to get into any specific details at the present time, it is important to keep in mind that by using so called intellectual arguments of various sorts, these men have shipwrecked the faith of many. Unfortunately, as it says in Jude 4, men have crept in unaware, and it is into our seminaries where they corrupt young minds, who go on to corrupt whole congregations.

But how do we know the bible is actually God's revelation to mankind? There are other religions in the world that have their own writings which they claim to be truths which God or a higher power revealed to them. Probably the two most well-known ones are the Quran or Koran and the Book of Mormon. There are others out there as well, some of which are reported to be as old as the bible, so how do we distinguish between them, if they all claim to be true, yet contradict one another? One of the ways we can do this is to look at the way in which they came to be revealed in the first place.

Islam believes that the Quran was verbally given by God (Allah) to the prophet Muhammad by the angel Gabriel and likewise the Book of Mormon was given to Joseph Smith by the angel Moroni, and in some circles is known as another testament of Jesus Christ. Hinduism has a large number of writings, but it is difficult to determine who wrote them. Now whether these writings were actually given to these men by angels, or demons, or perhaps their imagination spurred on by a piece of undigested cheese, we don't know, because it was given to one individual with nothing to prove their authenticity. But, given the benefit of doubt that they were given to them by God, you would expect that all the teachings would be the same, and if not, there must be a plurality of gods. But since they don't agree, something must be wrong.

However, the bible that Christians have as their authoritative revelation from God was written over a period of about 1500 years by a variety of writers from all walks of life. It contains 66 books, 39 written before the time of Jesus, which we call the Old Testament, and the 27 written after the death and resurrection of Jesus which we call the New Testament. And while these separate books have different authors given at different times throughout history, they have a common thread running throughout, and that is how God is dealing or relating to man. Why these books are chosen and others not, refer to the canonicity of scripture. But we are getting somewhat sidetracked from this day's article.

But we cannot forget that one of the most convincing realities that the bible is actually the revealed word of God, is fulfilled prophecies. Many prophecies were specifically given many decades, sometimes centuries before they occurred, some in quite detailed fashion. Some are so detailed that critics have assumed that they were written after the fact, and do their best to come up with theories to back their claims up. The field of apologetics has done much to answer these criticisms as well as many others, so for those interested in greater clarification of what we have been talking about, that would be a great place to start.

Fulfilled prophecy should be a sufficient reason in itself to distinguish it from all others, but there are two other reasons we want to mention in passing before moving on. The first being, that the scriptures themselves declare that they are the word of God. We have our verse we used at the beginning of this chapter, but there are numerous others, especially in the Old Testament, which have as a statement, "thus saith the Lord.", or something similar. While this argument has some problems, the second one doesn't, and that is that scripture is spiritually discerned to be the truth. 1 Corinthians 2:14 informs us that the "natural man" those who have not been regenerated or born again, "does not receive the things of the Spirit of God, for they are foolishness to him; nor can he know them, because they are spiritually discerned." As such, there is no way that we can "prove" these are the actual words of God, but can only do our duty and declare them to be so. To quote the Westminster Confession of Faith, "our full persuasion and assurance of the infallible truth and divine authority thereof, is from the inward work of the Holy Spirit bearing witness by and with the Word in our hearts."-Chap.1-5

Because of the truths and inerrancy we find in the Word of God, it must be our final authority when it concerns anything to do with God and His plan of salvation, and how we are to live our lives. To not believe in inerrancy is just a tool for unregenerate man to mold God into his image rather than to believe that we were CREATED in His image. If our articles do not conform to the truths we find in scripture, then they are just a waste of ink or as it were, computer bytes. That is why we always encourage our readers to check these things out. Because we usually only scratch the surface on many of these doctrines, it would do a Christian good to become more familiar with them, especially on this one, the inerrancy of God's word.

Christians contend that the bible is the only revelation which God has given to mankind in order for us to know who He is and who we are in relation to Him, and it begins it that wonderful declaration "In the beginning God created the Heavens and the Earth"-Genesis 1:1. Think on that, and until the next time we meet, Shalom.

BY GOOD AND NECESSARY CONSEQUENCE

"He must not acquire many horses for himself or cause the people to return to Egypt in order to acquire many horses."- Duet. 17:16 (ESV)

(This was written a while back in response to a question we had received concerning gambling, and since in a roundabout way it is an example of what we looked at last time we decided to include it here; some truths are spiritually discerned.)

In chapter one, part six of the Westminster Confession of Faith we read, "The whole counsel of God, concerning all things necessary for His own glory, man's salvation, faith and life, is either expressly set down in Scripture, or by good and necessary consequence may be deduced from Scripture...Nevertheless we acknowledge the inward illumination of the Spirit of God to be necessary for the saving understanding of such things as are revealed in the Word..."

Without going into great detail, the context of our verse is that the King of Israel was not to look for help from Egypt in time of war, hence the horses, but was to rely on the Lord God. He was also not to acquire great wealth for himself or many wives, but to be satisfies with what the Lord gave him.

What we are to do is to deduce principals from the word of God, or the Bible, and apply them to our lives. However, experience tells us that people are constantly asking if it is okay to (fill in the blank) if the bible doesn't expressly forbid it, even though it is forbidden by clear inference. It is only by the Spirit of God that any doctrine can or will be understood.

We read in 1 Corinthians 2:14 that "The natural person does not accept the things of the Spirit of God, for they are folly to him, and he is not able to understand them because they are spiritually discerned." (ESV) In other words, a non-Christian thinks that what the bible has to say is foolishness and will not understand unless the Holy Spirit teaches them. By understanding, I mean believe. When we believe something to be true, we act accordingly, otherwise we don't really believe it, or think it isn't important. But when God tells us truth and we don't act accordingly, then we are in complete disobedience. To know to do something or not to do something and then to act otherwise is sin. (James 4:17) It is nothing more than unbelief.

Because of this, we should not think it strange if those caught up in sin or a particular sin don't believe us when we point it out, and as usually is the case, want to argue their point. Perhaps they think that if they happen to win an argument with you, they have proved their case against God. Really they should be bringing their case to God in the first place, not to fallible men.

Jonathan Edwards, that great preacher and theologian from the past, said something that is very applicable for all times. "It is very common among men when they are strongly enticed to some sinful practice by their worldly interests or by their carnal appetites, to pretend that they do not think there is any evil in it, when indeed they know better." I think we have all had that attitude at one point or another.

Now getting back to Corinthians 2, we read in v.11, that we cannot know what the thoughts or motivations of another person is, meaning their will, but likewise it is possible that the individual does not intellectually know what motivates his will. But, whatever he or she most desires at the moment, will be what they will to do, which can be seen in manifest actions. So if a Christian sins, especially knowingly, it is a sign that at that moment they desire to be disobedient to their Savior; they want to temporarily dissolve that communion they have with Christ.

However, sometimes Christians sin unknowingly, yet in either case it is a sin. So what are we to think? In the first instance, when they come to their senses, there is need for confession and repentance, and a need to examine WHY they wanted to be disobedient. John Owen said it rightly, that "The deeds of the flesh are to be mortified in their CAUSES from whence they spring." But since that isn't the main point of this article, we won't delve into the various causes, except to say the lust of the eyes, the pride of life, and the desires of the flesh all need to be fought against.

In the second case a Christian sins but doesn't know it. Yet, it is still a sin, so what do we say? We must never forget that great exchange that Jesus' sacrifice accomplished for those that believe. He took our sin and guilt upon Himself, and in exchange clothed us in His perfect righteousness. So no matter what we do, we cannot lose that righteousness that we have obtained by faith; the gift given us by God.

However, as Paul the apostle says on more than one occasion and in different ways, do not use this liberty we have as a cloak for sin. Willful continued sin and disobedience usually reveals an unregenerate heart, though as our confessions say, sometimes a Christian may fall into prolonged and heinous practices.

But to return to our natural man, the man who is not a Christian, whatever he most desires, that is what motivates his will, whether he understands why or not. Where we as Christians come into conflict with them is when we condemn or perhaps the better word is expose their darling sins, lusts and practices as wrong.

One of the first things mentioned, and we have all heard it, is "don't judge me." Often times that passage in Matthew chapter 7 is brought up. Judge not, or condemn not, lest you be judged. There is a great difference between judging or condemning someone and confronting them with their sin. At the same time, we must not confront them in a condemning way. We must act in a way that shows our concern for their spiritual well-being. We are not trying to win an argument, but to show them spiritual truths for the good of their soul.

With all that being said, we get to our topic today, and that is on gambling. As there is no specific prohibition per se in the Bible, many have come to the conclusion that it is okay in moderation or as a form of entertainment. But if we are honest, the conclusion by good and necessary consequence is that it is an activity that we should not be participating in. Since there are a multitude of areas in which we might gamble, such as sports, lottery type venues, games of skill, (this is an area of great interest, because is it gambling when chance is not involved? We are not going to address this today, but it is a problematic question for a lot of people.) Casino type games and we could go on. But we are going to narrow it down to casino games, since that is probably the one that is most prevalent, and also where many of those other types might be participated in.

For the most part society has always recognized the perpetual harm in gambling, but in recent decades it has become more socially acceptable, and why is that? Likewise, as it has become more socially acceptable, it has increasingly become more legalized. There are some of us who are quite aware of this. The only reason it has become legalized is in order for government at all levels to profit from it. As it is disbursed among entities within the government system there will be individuals within the government who profit greatly. But we cannot forget that though government gets a share of the proceeds, the vast majority will go to the casino and its owners.

But, there is no social benefit to legalized gambling. True there are some jobs created, and wealth or income is redistributed, but not in a godly way. It is sometimes difficult to write a short article on such a topic because it delves into so many other aspects, such as the one we just mentioned, but we must move on, leaving this facet for another time. Legalized gambling is really no more than a form of taxation, but who is paying, and who is benefiting?

Something to remember in all this and that is what is the primary function of government? Does gambling promote that function or hinder it? God gave us or established for us government, and gave it for the benefit of all. Does gambling benefit all or some? But first things first, what is gambling? Perhaps the best definition is to play games of chance for money. As was mentioned earlier, there are other forms of gambling. Some people use the stock market to gamble, but as mentioned before, let's stick to casino games.

Whatever game it is, the casino always has an advantage, so whatever that percentage is, that is how much you are giving away each time the cards are dealt, or the dice thrown, or the machine played. But as a Christian, how are we to address this? Some people use this as a form of recreation, or so they say, and it is no different than a golfer who spends money on green fees, clubs, and all the other expenses associated with the game of golf. And you know what, they are right if they are solely using it as a form of recreation, but let's get real. If there wasn't an opportunity of gain playing these games of chance, nobody would play. As an aside, that doesn't mean that golfers and others who spend money on their particular escape from reality are off the hook. It can be just as destructive as gambling, but since it is socially acceptable, it is perceived as okay. Perhaps we will address this some other day.

The actual problem of gambling is spiritually discerned and if someone is using it for entertainment, then we must ask in what way are they being entertained? Is this a form of entertainment that God approves of, and what is it that God does approve of? Beyond that, why are casinos built? Bottom line, is so the owners can gain that percentage of money from the players each time they bet. Now we all acknowledge that sometimes someone will hit it big, and there are others who actually win something, but whose money was it? The answer most often given is from the casino, but in fact it has come from the numerous other players; the house or casino just takes their cut of the proceeds, which often times amounts to quite a lot.

When God created man in His image, is this the kind of thing He had in mind? Of course not. Everyone was to work, and if someone needed anything it was provided. If I grew grapes and you grew tomatoes, we would share that all would have some, but that was the ideal that never happened. When the knowledge of good and evil entered the world, and men became sinners and had to work by the sweat of their brow, some found it easier to invent ways of evil to take what belonged to another. Cheating, stealing, murder, lying and all other sorts of gimmicks were used in order to escape that punishment of hard unsatisfying work. It is a whole lot easier if I let you do all the work, and then take it from you. We see this played out on a daily basis by the individual all the way up to governments. But, this is not what God intended when He first made man.

Almost all of us know someone who has lost it all by gambling, and if we don't personally know someone, we are probably acquainted with someone who does. They have not only lost all their resources, but their families, job, and reputation, because they went from recreational gamblers to addicts. And what determines that one spin that causes them to cross the line? As is often the case in addiction to anything, other forms of addiction are taken up in order to silence that shout of desperation that comes from the soul. Though it is only a small percentage who become addicts, there are many millions more who actually gamble, and for the most part lose. But let's assume for arguments sake, that the vast majority of those who do gamble can afford to lose whatever they gamble. Couldn't this money be used for more important things, such as the relieving and bettering of someone else who really needs help?

A Christian knows that the most important thing in life is to love the Lord our God with all our heart, soul, strength and mind, and to love our neighbor as ourselves. This love is an unconditional love. It is a love which will do all you can for the well-being of another, regardless of the negative impact it might have on your welfare. This is a godly love, long suffering and enduring and very few if any of us have ever met anyone like that, except for Jesus. But, however difficult, it is something to strive for, and we can't be doing that if we are stewarding our resources in ungodly ways. It is like putting our money into bags with holes in them, and there will come a day of accountability. Yet despite all this, how many of us (Christians) are gambling in one form or another?

We have been separated out from the world by God. We are to be different, because we are different. That doesn't mean we don't associate with unbelievers, but it does mean that we don't participate in their sinful behaviors. Christians shouldn't be spending their time in casinos, doing those things that the rest of the world does, but I know many of us do.

Let's be honest for a second. Sin can be physically and mentally fun and entertaining. But as those who have put on Christ, having made a profession of faith, we are to forsake sin and to depart from the appearance of evil. If we don't, we are just facilitators of those who do sin. I'm not sure what the ramifications are for a Christian, but it should send tremors through us when we read, "Woe to them through whom they come (meaning temptations) It would be better for him if a milestone were hung around his neck and he were cast into the sea than he should cause one of these little ones to sin." (Luke 17:1-2) So if we gamble for whatever reason, and cause our brother to sin, what gives? All scripture is God breathed, but these are the direct words of God, our Savior Jesus Christ. Again, I have no idea of the ramifications, but if we have a genuine profession of faith in Jesus Christ, how can we cause another to sin?

Getting back to our subject, how are we to convince others that gambling is wrong? It was in a different context, but completely relevant to our topic, when John Calvin stated, "We must be unlike those whom we reprove, if we do not wish to expose our doctrine to ridicule, and to be reckoned impudent; and, on the other hand, when we serve God with a pure conscience, our doctrine obtains weight and authority, and holds even adversaries to be more fully convinced." Whether it is gambling or any other sin, no one is going to believe us when we say it is wrong if we are doing it ourselves.

There is much more that could be said on this subject, and what little we have said could be further clarified. Books could be written on the subject, but our objective was simply to reveal that gambling is wrong in so many ways. It is an activity that has not only been seen immoral historically, but also by facts of experience. At the same time, when it comes down to whether it is a sin or not, and whether it is addressed by God in His word, it is, but it must be spiritually discerned. It comes back full circle to or original passage in 1 Corinthians 2; the natural person cannot/will not understand. But for those who do understand and are still gambling from time to time, what are you doing? There is no need to address this any further, but get with God and repent and ask for guidance and deliverance.

To those of you who are what we call the natural man or in the flesh, what are you going to do? If God says this is wrong, or a sin, which can be easily deduced by scripture, what are you going to do? You really only have two choices, and that is to continue on in the course you have been living, or to turn to Jesus for the forgiveness of sin. Jesus was the only begotten Son of God, born of a virgin, lived a perfect life of sinless obedience, and was killed on the cross as a substitute for those who would believe in Him. It was for the punishment of our sin that He died, and the perfect life that He lived is accredited to all those who place their faith in Him. He was buried, and in three days rose again, ascended into heaven, and is returning again to judge those who are alive and those who are dead. There is eternal life by faith, but there is eternal wrath and punishment for those who refuse to be reconciled to God by faith in Christ. Death physically and eternally are the wages of sin given to those who don't repent and are pleased to continue a life of sin now.

What is your choice going to be? I present before you this day the choice of life and death. Today is the day of salvation, today is the day to admit you are a sinner and ask Jesus to forgive you for your sins and to save you. He gladly will and we implore you to be reconciled to God for eternal life. I know that many of you will not choose life, but remember these words thousands of ages from now. Thousands of years of ages from now when hope has died a million times and the torment is endless, remember that God came to you one day saying repent and be reconciled, and turn from your wicked ways, but you just wouldn't give up those temporary pleasures of sin.

So I set before you the ultimate gamble. Are you willing to gamble your eternal soul that I am wrong, that your sin is really nothing and that God doesn't care? In a way I am setting before you the perfect and ultimate 50-50 gamble. I am right or I am wrong. Read Blaise Pasqual's wager and see what you think. Again, we could go on for many pages, but it would be pointless. You have a choice this day, not tomorrow or sometime in the future; choose life.

For us who profess to be Christians, we must walk in a manner which proclaims who we are. When Jesus returns, will He find us faithful? Perhaps our life will amount to nothing more than wood, hay, stubble and dung. It is a little crass, and I won't spell it out, but your life has been a big pile of BS. We may be saved, but haven't lived much of a life that glorified God. It isn't too late to change that, so may each one of us examine ourselves and start walking in a way that glorifies God and proclaims who He is, and who we are, children of the Most High God; be salt and light.

"When I was a child, I spoke as a child, I understood as a child, I thought as a child; but when I became a man, I put away childish things."-1 Corinthians 13:11

Until we meet again, either in this life or in the one to come, Shalom.

P.S. Often times we are asked "where is it forbidden?" Our best response might be," where is it allowed?"

THE HOLINESS OF GOD

Earlier we asked the question, "are you saved?" and the response we might and should receive back is, "saved from what?" This is a very legitimate question which we intend to answer next time, but in order to do so, we need to know a little more about God. The very first verse in the bible is so important, but it is so familiar to Christians, that I am afraid we overlook its significance. So let's look at it for a minute. "In the beginning, God created the heavens and the earth."

For those of us who grew up in church, that is most likely the first verse you ever memorized. It tells us what we are, and that is a created being. Well, if that is the case, then who created us, and the answer is of course God. Very easy and elementary; we were created, and God created us. But, when something is created, it is created for a reason, so why did God create us, for what purpose were we created? Not such an easy question to answer, but we are given the clue or answer in that very first chapter in Genesis, verse 26-27. "Then God said 'Let us make man in our image, after our likeness'". It is important that we read to the end of the chapter in order to see what all we were created to do, but we mustn't overlook that statement "Let us". We will deal with it later, but since the bible teaches that there is only ONE God, who is this "Us"? And we continue on into verse 27 and it tells us that God created man (male and female) in his own image, in the image of God he created him. We might easier understand the word likeness; we were made like God. As long as we don't confuse the two, image and likeness, we'll be okay. Otherwise, we can easily fall into what so many pagan religions have done, and make God into someone who resembles us as we see ourselves.

Without getting bogged down in some other areas, let's just look at a few things that the bible says about who God is. We call these the attributes of God and we distinguish between what we call communicable and incommunicable attributes of God. This just means that when we consider the image of God in man, some attributes we don't have. For instance, the bible declares that God is omniscience, omnipotent, and omnipresent. This is just a fancy way of saying He is all knowing, all powerful, and all present. Now the word or prefix Omni, which signifies all, means in all ways and in all places. So when the bible says that God is all knowing, or omniscient, it means He knows all things about all things. We are always amazed at that individual who is so knowledgeable in his field of endeavor, especially those who are what we might call pioneers, yet God far out passes them. God knows everything there is to know about everything. Our minds can barely grasp that concept, and that is just one attribute of God.

Now it is easy to understand that there are certain attributes that God could not give to man. Self-existence would be one for example but we can easily come up with others. Since we have a body and exist in time, we cannot be omnipresent at all times; God is said to exist in eternity, in all places at all times, and our tongues may speak it, and our brain might believe it, but our mind cannot fully comprehend it. This is just one of those incommunicable attributes that we are talking about, but what of the communicable ones?

Being created in the image of God, we are going to naturally have some of the same attributes or characteristics. We have the capacity to know, to be known, to love, to be good or kind, as well as many other characteristics. As you can see, these tend to be moral type attributes. But we only have them to a certain degree, or a finite degree, where God's is infinite. For example, we can be good, but only in a certain way, and it is necessary we explain this a little bit so we don't get confused by the word "good". This seems to be deviating a little bit from our article today, but hopefully I can explain in it such a way as you can see how it ties into everything.

When God had finished creating everything at the end of the six days, He looked at it and saw that it was very good. We (mankind, represented by Adam) were very good; not partially, but fully good without knowing what evil was. What Adam did before the fall was good, because whatever he chose (willed) to do had no evil in it as evil had not yet been introduced into the world. But when he willingly chose to disobey God by eating from the Tree of the Knowledge of Good and Evil, not only did he commit evil and learn what evil is, but he spiritually died and became liable to physical death as well.

God created us with a body and a soul, and while these cannot be separated except by death, the soul is that part of us that is the image of God. By Adam's sin/disobedience that day, all mankind is subject to not only physical death, but is born spiritually dead, and as such, cannot do anything spiritually good. For example, say someone decides to finance the digging of water wells in drought ridden places in Africa in order that people might be able to grow food and live, we say that is a good thing. Outwardly it is, and it helps a great deal of people, but if it is not done with the intention of glorifying God, which someone who is spiritually dead cannot do, then spiritually speaking it is not good; it was done from some other motive.

Now our soul being made in the image of God is immortal in the sense that it will never cease to exist. Nevertheless, when separated from the body at death, it continues to will to do something, but being spiritually dead can only will that which is evil, not good, which brings us to the holiness of God. (We will talk about the body later, but we have already gone beyond what we had planned for the day and need to finish)

When we think of holy, we tend to think of some moral aspect, which is partially correct, but a better idea is that of being set apart from that which is ordinary. Now God is all of this to perfection. He is so morally pure and perfect in His nature, that the angels say Holy, Holy, Holy, a perfection of set apartness that cannot be totally comprehended by the human mind; we don't have the words to describe it. Because of this, no imperfection or impurity of whatever kind can commune or dwell or come into the presence of this Holy God. So how can a soul which is no longer good, can no longer do that which is right (it is unrighteous) that is spiritually dead, come before God, and if not, what are the ramifications? We will try and answer that next time, and until then, Shalom.

THE SPIRITUALLY DEAD SOUL

We mentioned last time and briefly touched on the holiness of God and the spiritually dead soul. The question we asked then was how can a spiritually dead soul, unrighteous and no longer good or holy, come before a holy God and what are the ramifications of that? Now in a nutshell, this is what the entire bible is about. It answers how a sinful man can be reconciled to God, and how He has been working this out in history. So let's look first at some of the consequences concerning the soul that is not reconciled to God.

Sometimes when writing these articles, I feel like in many ways I am doing a disservice to the reader by not going into more details on certain subjects. One such time would be our last article on the holiness of God. Many fine and detailed books have been written on the subject and yet we only devoted a few sentences on it. Such is the dilemma of writing short pieces. But if we can just begin to glimpse the utter perfection of God's holiness or set apartness, we shall see that this applies to His whole Being, not just a part.

Oftentimes we speak of the simplicity of God, and this just means that He is not composed of parts. We use the term attributes or characteristics of God in order that we can understand them, and when God speaks to us through His word, He uses as I think John Calvin said, baby talk. God speaks to us in a way that our human minds can somewhat comprehend what goes far beyond our capabilities. So when we describe God and say that He is loving, truthful, omniscience, and holy, along with all the rest of the attributes, we mustn't think that sometimes He is one, sometimes another, but that they are all working (terrible wording) simultaneously to their perfection; He is always on display in His fullness. This is what I use for my definition of the glory of God. It is the brilliant refulgence of all His attributes working together simultaneously. That is why we sometimes see writers break out into doxology, especially the apostle

Paul, because the simple contemplation of it all is so wondrous. Now part of God's holiness concerns His justice.

We all have a pretty good idea of what justice is, but sometimes using dictionary meanings clarify it for us. One of these meanings is getting a reward or penalty as deserved. That intimates that there is some rule or law that must be followed or obeyed in order to receive a reward, and if not followed a penalty. So if we obey we are doing right, or being righteous, and will receive the reward, but if we don't obey, in other words break the law, we deserve and will receive the punishment. Another definition is the use of authority to uphold what is just, and also the administration of law.

God's perfect righteousness by which we mean He can do nothing that is not perfectly right, demands that He properly reward or punish those who uphold or break His law; it is the perfectly right thing to do. To not do so would be an unrighteous act which is impossible for God, since he is perfectly righteous. We don't want to chase our tail here, but God cannot not reward the righteous, likewise He cannot not punish the one who disobeys the law. (I know I used a couple of double negatives, but there is a reason why; it makes the reader look twice.) One of mankind's problems are that he wants to be rewarded for doing that which is right, but not punished for doing what is wrong. We all have a tendency to be like that, but a perfectly righteous being like God is not. As the lawgiver and the administrator of the law He must be righteous and give out rewards and punishments as merited. Looking again at that spiritually dead soul that will not be reconciled to God, what must be the consequences, the righteous thing to be done?

The righteous thing that must be done is to incur the penalty for the law that was broken. To not receive that penalty would be an act of unrighteousness, and God being perfectly just in all He does, must as Judge, apply the penalty to the wrongdoer. It is important here that we realize that everyone is born guilty, spiritually dead, and liable to the wrath of God, an eternal punishment against those who are eternally guilty. There are so many verses we could look at in the book of Romans alone, especially in the first six chapters, that would make this very clear, and we encourage you to read them, but we will just pick a few and you can read the rest later.

"Therefore, as through one man's offense judgement came to all men, resulting in condemnation..."-Rom. 5:18

"But in accordance with your hardness and your unrepentant heart you are treasuring up for yourself wrath in the day of wrath and revelation of the righteous judgement of God, who will render to each one according to his deeds: eternal life to those who by patient continuance in doing good seek for glory, honor and immortality; but to those who are self-seeking and do not obey the truth, but obey unrighteousness-indignation and wrath, tribulation and anguish, on every soul of man who does evil..."-Rom. 2:5-9

Like I said, read those first few chapters of Romans, and it will become crystal clear the predicament and destiny of the spiritually dead soul. It is to spend eternity enduring the wrath of God against its sin in hell, the lake of fire and brimstone prepared for the devil and his angels. That is mentioned in Matthew 25, but we also read in Revelation 20, that the devil, the false prophet and beast are there being tormented day and night forever and ever, as well as those whose names are not written in the Book of Life. It is often asked if this is a literal lake of fire and brimstone that the ungodly will be tormented in forever, and there is no reason not to take it literally, but something to consider is that some have reasoned that it is much worse than that and is much worse than our minds could comprehend, fire being the worst imaginable. Until we know otherwise, let's not speculate, but let God speak for Himself. He has declared it to be a lake of fire and brimstone where the ungodly will spend eternity being tormented day and night forever and ever, so we proclaim it to be so.

This is the wrath of God against sin perfectly displayed. Each one of us was born guilty, having the sin of Adam imputed to us, spiritually dead, physically dying, with no desire or ability to do good, or desire to seek God. Though we know He exists, as even the heavens declare the glory and being of God, yet the thoughts and intents of our hearts is continuously evil. Hell is the destiny each and every one of us was born into and unless something changes, it cannot be escaped; we need someone to save us.

Previously we have mentioned that salvation comes by faith in Jesus Christ, and though we don't go into detail every article, we do try to remind the reader in order that they might examine themselves as to whether they are saved or not. Which brings us to one of the questions we raised earlier, and one in which we need to be able to answer when proclaiming the gospel. When someone asks us why they need to be saved, but especially saved from what, we need to be prepared to answer. We are saved from the wrath of God.

By faith in Christ we are saved not only from the wrath of God, but can now come before God clothed in the righteousness of Christ, His life and death imputed to us. A spiritually dead soul, unrighteous and no longer holy must be made alive again, born again, recreated as it were, a new creation, in order to come into the presence of a holy God. By faith in Christ, all this has happened, and we will look at it more in upcoming articles.

As Christians, we have been saved to and for the praise of God's glorious grace, so I ask myself as well as you, are you doing so? Until next time, Shalom.

BLINDED MINDS

(This was originally written sometime in 2020, and in it we reference an individual who according to a news article, made some claims about God that were false. If his words were taken out of context, we apologize now for anything negative we may have said. We did not try to contact him.)

We see many evils in this world, the covid-19 virus being one of them, and now that we live in a world of mass communication, it seems more prevalent. Not that the degree to which evil exists or manifests itself is any greater, but we see it more often. In addition to the ability to see it, there are more people populating the world today, so it is only natural that more will be going on. But there is an even greater evil going on which very few are aware of, and that is the evil of having our minds blinded to the truth; spiritual truth.

Some of you have probably read or heard of all the conspiracy theories concerning this event they call a pandemic, but I am going to disappoint you if you think that is what we are going to talk about. It does have some relevance to what we are looking at, but principally in that it has given opportunity to those who are deceptors or deceivers. Now there are several topics which are related to what we will be looking at today, and while we may touch on all of them, spiritual deception is principally what we will look at.

Looking briefly at a few verses found in 2 Corinthians 4, we see that spiritual agendas have changed little over the centuries from when this was written. We are going to paraphrase this a little, but read chapter 4:1-7. There are men out there, who abide in the hidden things of dishonesty, and they walk craftily or scheming, and they handle the word of God deceitfully. Now men who do these types of things are the pawns of Satan, who is called the god of this world, and he uses them to blind the minds of them which do not believe. And what is it that they do not believe? They do not believe the gospel, and he blinds their minds lest the gospel of the glory of Christ who is the image of God should shine unto them. And where do we find these men? Unfortunately we find them in pulpits all across the land and world, spewing forth their blasphemies and profanities, but typically they learn this in their seminaries. We are going to address one of those in a moment, but let us continue.

True preachers or ministers do not preach themselves, or their opinions, but they preach Jesus Christ, and Him crucified. They do not preach about the word of God, but they preach the word of God. There is a big difference there. A characteristic of true preachers is v.6 in our passage. "For God, who commanded the light to shine out of darkness, has shined in our hearts, to give the light of the knowledge of the glory of God in the face of Jesus Christ." There is a lot in that sentence to think about, but it differentiates those who proclaim truth and those who don't. When teaching or preaching, there are many, many topics from which to choose from. And while it is useful and necessary to be diversified (for there is no other way to know God, without utilizing the whole of scripture which is His revelation unto mankind) at the end of the day, it is about proclaiming the light of the knowledge of the glory of God in the face of Jesus Christ. So because Jesus is God or Lord, (is it really necessary to defend that statement to those reading this? If so ask, and we will get around to it again as it has been done in times past) any distortion or misrepresentation of Jesus is a misrepresentation of God, and a misrepresentation of God is a misrepresentation of Jesus; Jesus is LORD.

Now because of this corona virus being a pandemic and all, many ideas have made their way into the mainstream of media that normally would not be heard. Though thousands upon thousands of people die each year from the common flu or cancer or heart disease, not to mention drunk driving and abortions, most governments for the most part turn a blind eye. It is hard not to start thinking conspiracy, but there are some who think this is a judgement from God. In certain respects it is, but whether this is a direct special judgement, I will not speculate. But it has brought it to our attention that death is real, and that most people are scared to death of it. Perhaps this is a final appeal from a loving God who says He has no pleasure in the death of the wicked. A time for repentance. The story of Jonah and the Ninevites comes to mind; but will we heed the warning?

But it is at precisely this moment when the blasphemers and those who profane God come in, and say peace peace, when there is no peace. Now it is perhaps harsh in calling these people blasphemers and profaners, and if so, apologies. But at the end of days, and truly all those in between, when God sends judgement upon the world, men are said to blaspheme the name of God and not repent. Looking at dictionary meanings always seems to bring clarity, so let us look at them. Profane is to show disrespect or contempt for sacred things, and blasphemy is profane speech, writing or action concerning God or sacred things. So is speaking in a way which diminishes from the attributes of God blasphemy? Distorting who He is by emphasizing one attribute over another? (By that we mean saying such things as God is love, but not a God of justice.) Of course it is, whether intentional or not. And this brings us to my concern, and it is those people who get attention in the media for supposedly being "religious authorities" when they are in fact angels of Satan.

Recently I read an article on the internet from USA Today entitled "Coronavirus and God: What Faith leaders say about Pandemic." It was on the internet again today, and it is so irritating that I could not let it slide. First of all, they are not leaders. Except for the realm that they travel in they are not necessarily known. No one that I am acquainted with has ever heard of these persons. Secondly, there is only ONE God, and while there might be many "faiths" out there, there is only one that has any true relevance. Why were the Pastafarians not represented in this article? Now admittedly, there are many more Muslims then there are Pastafarians, (make no mistake, we meant Pasta, not Rasta) but in the end scheme of things their religions are nothing more than deceptions. False religions have caused untold problems throughout history and one only has to look at what happened to Roman Catholicism and the inquisitions to see just one example, but it gets worse. The greatest deceptions have come in the guise of twisting the nature of God, which is why we call it blasphemy.

One of these so called leaders of faith in the article was "A Christian theologian, author and teacher at Northwestern Nazarene University in Nampa, Idaho." Now what he teaches and what he has authored, I never bothered to find out, and if the article in question has taken his quotes and comments out of context then an apology is extended. The media loves to distort the truth, fake news and all, which is why we will not mention his name, but if the shoe fits, is not he a disciple of the evil one himself? But since he is not the only one that has spoken in such ways, we will give him the benefit of doubt, and as is the case in all such things, let God judge him. It is not our place to do so, but we can judge of what he says.

It is his contention that God is a God of love, and this is very true. But, we must define what love is, not based on man's conception of what it is, but how God Himself defines it. Also, we cannot let one attribute of God, quench all others. Is not God a God of justice as well? And, if God is not just, then how can He be good? And, of course if he is not good, then how can he love? We also say He is omnipotent or all powerful, and as such, could he not prevent evil, the virus in particular? Could we not say that He is lovingly allowing this virus to be a means of justice against our evils in order to turn our hearts to him in repentance in order that we may be saved from the wrath to come? This virus is insignificant in what is to come. This man who is assumed to be a teacher of theology as the article insinuates, does not think that God allows evil to happen, but he proposes an alternative proposition, one straight from the mouth of Satan. The article in question says, "He (the person we are talking about) doesn't buy any of those. In his teachings, he presents a fourth option: God can't simply prevent the coronavirus – or any other natural evils – singlehandedly but requires "our participation and cooperation" to fight it," Again, I hope this person has been taken out of context, which happens a lot, but it is representative of a lot of teaching which goes by the name of "Christian."

But this distorts God and all that He has revealed of Himself in the Holy Scriptures. If this man were truly a theologian, and I believe he is, (we are all theologians to a certain extent) he would know that God cannot be split into pieces. We have fancy words for this, but it amounts to the fact that all of God's attributes work together and they do so simultaneously. It is the simplicity of God, in that it is one. We separate them sometimes in order to explain them, but they in fact all work together, to display the glory of God. This cannot be over emphasized enough, but all that happens is to display the glory of God. Justice, mercy, grace, wrath, love, law, omnipresence, omnipotence, omniscience, and all the other attributes of God are all working together simultaneously in order that the refulgence of the glory of God might be manifested, and it is done so in the knowledge of the glory of God in the face of Jesus Christ.

This is why the evil one uses men such as this to distort or profane God in ways that blind our minds to the truth of who God is. God is all loving, and as such has sent his only begotten son into the world that whosoever would believe on him would have eternal life. And God demonstrates this love, because justice demands that evil be punished. And the essence of evil is that all have sinned and fallen short of the glory of God which demands perfection. But if the evil one can get your mind blinded from the truth of all this, you will perish, which is what the evil one wants. This is why men such as this are disgusting, in that they pervert the truth and draw men away from the gospel, they blind their minds.

Now we have gone on and on here and truly this is only a fraction of what I would say against those who would distort the truth of God, but we must close. Already I can see that this is almost double what we would normally post, yet it is all so incomplete. As you can also see, this corona virus is a time to focus our attention on what is most important. And this most important thing is knowing God and enjoying Him forever, but how many of you know what that means? In a nut shell, God is reconciling the world to Himself through Jesus, and Jesus was the substitutionary and atoning sacrifice, through which this was done. Believe in the Lord Jesus Christ and you will be saved.

Has your mind been blinded by the God of this world? Has something other than the truth been presented to your mind which resembles light, but is really darkness? If the light that is in you be darkness, how great is that darkness. Many minds are blinded by the god of this world, and it is our prayer that you would not let this time of fear and panic further blind you, but that God would enlighten you into repentance of heart, and that the glory of God as seen in the gospel of Jesus might shine in your hearts.

We live in a time of great spiritual darkness, and yet sometimes God sends a great sign of lovingkindness and wrath in one event in order to get our attention so that we might amend our ways. And in saying all this, it is only to draw your attention to the only salvation, and that is through faith in the finished work of Jesus. Much of what we have said here today, needs to be expanded on, and if there is anything you need clarity on, please ask and we will try and answer. But above all, do not let your minds be further blinded from the truth. Do not let those men who would distort God into their own image, those ambassadors of the evil one, captivate you with words which appeal to your pleasure. Do not deceive yourself with the philosophy of men, but listen to the words of Jesus himself, "Those who come to me I will in no way cast out."

It is time to close, though reluctantly as this is so incomplete, but until next time, Shalom.

THE BREVITY OF LIFE AND ITS MEANINGLESS APART FROM GOD

Last time we considered how blinded we are to spiritual realities that are going on all around us on a constant basis. There are a variety of reasons, one of the main ones being that the evil one, Satan, the god of this present age, distracts us in various ways in order to keep us from seeing truth. This is done in such a multitude of ways that it is almost impossible to name them all, but we could probably sum them up in three ways; the desires of the flesh, the desires of the eyes, and the pride of life. Now the pursuit of these desires distracts us from one of the most important realities we have to face, and that is that life is short, you're going to die, and that life is meaningless apart from God. We chase things and become addicted to various activities and sometimes substance abuse, in order to silence our conscience and God. We know, whether we admit it or not, that this life is completely devoid of meaning if there isn't a God, but we also know there is a God. We may not want to admit it, but subconsciously we all know there is a God, but as the bible teaches us, we are at enmity with God. We have a hatred for Him, even if we don't know it, and until that changes we will constantly be chasing after the things of this world.

Two roads diverged in a yellow wood,
And sorry I could not travel both
And be one traveler, long I stood
And looked down one as far as I could
To where it bent in the undergrowth;

Then took the other, as just as fair,
And having perhaps the better claim,

Because it was grassy and wanted wear;
Though as for that the passing there
Had worn them really about the same,

And both that morning equally lay
In leaves no step had trodden black.
Oh, I kept the first for another day!
Yet knowing how way leads on to way,
I doubted if I should ever come back.

I shall be telling this with a sigh
Somewhere ages and ages hence:
Two roads diverged in a wood, and I-
I took the one less traveled by,
And that has made all the difference.

Every time I read this poem by Robert Frost, I come away with a sense of loneliness, sadness and regret. Perhaps the path we have chosen in life has turned out fine, but there is always that foreboding and nagging thought, of what if. What if we had never moved, would our life be as fulfilling? There are friends lost to the memories of time. We shall never see them again. How did life turn out for them, will I see them in heaven? Those things we always intended to do, but never will have time for. I always wanted to play the violin, but it seems like it will never come to pass. Those places we wanted to visit. We know deep down that it's never going to happen. Sometimes there is a sadness and futility to it all, and we come away thinking to ourselves that life is meaningless and what's the point.

And then I remember.

"Fear God and keep His commandments, for this is the whole duty of man." Ecclesiastes12:13. (ESV)

This is the meaning of life. Lifetimes of philosophers have come and gone, searching for the meaning of existence, but for the most part, their search has been futile. Our lives in many respects are spent in this same search, trying to fill an emptiness that we feel inside. Trying to find significance, trying to fulfill that cry of the soul which shakes its fist at God, and says I will be like the most high. Proving that enmity against God we were all born with. We have forgotten that we were created, and are not self-existent, and as such were created with a specific purpose in mind. TO GLORIFY GOD.

Life is but a vapor, a shadow passing away under a cloudy sky, a fog dissipated by the rising sun, and though a man is given 70 or 80 years on this earth, it passes by as a stranger in the night. The brevity of it catches our breath, and unless one understands the meaning of life, it will all be vanity, or meaningless. We find our true happiness and fulfillment in glorifying God in whatever our hands find to do.

When I was young, I was shown the meaning of life, but knowing it and living it are two different things, and as we grow older, many of the things we have been taught by God through the Holy Scriptures become quite clear, as many of you could attest to. However, because we are so prone to forgetfulness, not from old age, but from the distractions of the world and everyday life, it is necessary to be reminded of certain things from time to time. The Apostle Peter thought it necessary to stir up our lethargic minds in order that we would remember truth, because we are so prone to forget that we have been cleansed from our old sins. So with that in mind, today we are going to be looking in the last part of Ecclesiastes, verses 5, 7-8 in chapter 11, and all of 12 except 9-12. (Read)

Ecclesiastes traditionally has been ascribed as written by Solomon, the son of David, King of Israel, and to him it has been said he is the wisest man who ever lived. This was probably written in his old age, after a lifetime of searching out the meaning of life, and after all was done, v. 13 says it all. We know the end of Solomon didn't end well, and I think 12:1 has a dual purpose here. One, that we remember our creator before it's too late, but two, that the years Solomon had left were spent in a futility of mind, a certain resignation that he had not remembered his Creator, and he had no pleasure in the years that remained.

For the most part we think of Solomon in a good light, but the warning he gives us here sounds like the one of whom it is too late for repentance, the judgement has come, and he wants us to take heed lest we fall also.

Turn to 1Kings11:1-13. (Read)

Sometimes I get sorrowful, or maybe a hurt in the pit of my stomach, when I read of men like this that fall from the grace of God. God had done amazing things for Solomon, and yet look at what he did. But, we hear of the same sort of things happening in our day, with men of reputation for godliness falling into gross sin. And though maybe not to the same degree, do we not commit sin, even after becoming Christians. We are reminded in the Westminster confession of Faith concerning perseverance that those whom God has saved will never fall away from that state of grace, yet, they may through the temptations of Satan and of the world, the remains of corruption still within us, and neglecting those means by which we persevere, fall into grievous sins. This causes us to grieve the Holy Spirit, have our hearts and consciences wounded and hardened, and come to be deprived of the assurance of those graces and comforts we have in Christ.

"Remember now your Creator in the days of your youth, before the difficult days come, and the years draw near when you say 'I have no pleasure in them'"- Eccl. 12:1

We can look at this in two ways, the primary one being to remember God while you are young. As we grow older and the everyday pressures of life bear down on us, the less likely we are to think about God, religion and the things concerning our need of salvation; and then we get old. It happens quickly as many of you in this room can attest to. (This was originally a message given in a nursing home.) We can't see or hear well, food doesn't taste as good anymore, we become weak, and there is no pleasure to life. But there is still a little time left to remember our creator, yet it is imperative we do so before death. For then the dust, our body will return to the earth and the spirit or soul will return to God who gave it. Then that verse which I am fixing to tell you will render you speechless if you have not remembered your Creator by turning to Him by faith in Jesus Christ. "It is appointed once unto a man to die, but after that, the judgement."-(Hebrews 9:27) Are you ready to meet God, to stand before Him on that day of judgement?

But, we are also to remember the God of our youth. Many of you grew up in Christian families, and were perhaps saved at an early age. Others in junior high or high school, maybe even college, but regardless of when, you had years of instruction in righteousness and godliness when you were young. As you grew older did you remember and follow these teachings? How about now that there are only days or months left? It is sad and regrettable that we know or hear of so many that strayed away from the faith by neglecting to remember their Creator.

Such is the life of Solomon, and he gives us a great example of what can happen to the wisest of us, the richest of us, to those close to God, if they fail to remember God. (Read 1 Kings 9:1-9)We read earlier in 1 Kings 11 of the idolatry and evil that Solomon committed, but God had specifically warned him NOT to do what he eventually did. The reason he turned to idolatry is that he loved many foreign women, beginning by marrying the daughter of Pharaoh. Israel had been strictly forbidden to intermarry with foreigners, for this very reason. We also read that this happened when he was old. There is no reason to think that this idolatry came about all of a sudden, but was probably a result of Solomon increasingly turning his back on God.

We are not going to go over them, but there were severe consequences that were going to happen to Israel because of what Solomon did. It is so easy for us to forget that our sin, whether small or great has consequences that not only affect us, but perhaps numerous others that we haven't even considered. The emptiness of life without God and of forgetting God is summed up in this lament of Solomon, "Vanity of vanities, All is vanity" What a peril it is to forget our Creator.

Remember now your Creator. As mentioned earlier, many of you here today are living v.2-5. Your mind is still sharp, but the body is beginning to grow weary. It's harder to see, especially without glasses, and the muscles of the body just don't cooperate as they used to. Sleep doesn't seem so restful anymore, and all our desires for the things of life have diminished. But, you are here today to remember your Creator, to worship Him in song and prayer and in the fellowship of His word. You are here to thank Him for all He has done for us in the work of His Son Jesus.

Remember now your Creator. Remember Him before that silver cord which unites the body and soul is removed. Remember Him before the brain no longer functions. Remember Him before the heart stops beating. Remember Him now.

Remember what He said to you in your youth through Christ. "I am the way, the truth and the life; no one comes to the Father but by me." (John14:6) And "that no one can come to Me unless it has been granted to him by My Father." (John6:65)

"And this is the will of Him who sent Me, that everyone who sees the Son and believes in Him may have everlasting life; and I will raise him up at the last day". (John6:40)

Remember what Peter said through the Holy Spirit on the day of Pentecost. "Repent and be baptized in the name of Jesus Christ for the forgiveness of sins; and you shall receive the gift of the Holy Spirit. For the promise is to you and to your children, and to all who are afar off, as many as the Lord our God will call." (Acts2:38-39)

Remember your Creator now, before the dust of the body returns to the earth, and the Spirit returns to God who gave it. "It is appointed for a man once to die and after that the judgement." (Heb.9:27)

Remember all the endeavors of this life time are meaningless apart from a relationship with God through Jesus Christ. Try as we might, through activities, addictions, distractions and everything else that the world might throw our way, nothing will stifle that voice of God that asks as it did of Adam in the Garden of Eden, "Where are you?"

God knows where you are, but, and it's a big BUT, do you know where you are? Are you walking hand in hand with God in the cool of the day communing with him, being reconciled to Him by Jesus, or are you still at enmity with Him? This word enmity doesn't just mean an enemy, but it is a deep seated seething hatred. This is the ultimate sinfulness of sin. We don't have time to get into all the aspects of it, but sin is that separation of God from man, spiritual death. Our whole duty was but to obey His command, yet in Adam we sinned. The outward sins we commit, are just manifestations of hatred we have against God and His ways, and against our fellow man that dwells on this earth with us. Because of this hatred and spiritual deadness and separation, we have somehow gotten the notion that we are masters of our own destiny; we have forgotten we are just created beings, created for the glorification of God. And though we were created for His glory, and God is Sovereign, yet He has created us in His image as responsible beings. We do not have time today to properly expound Gods sovereignty and man's responsibility, but never forget that our fall from grace in Adam in no way abrogated or diminished our responsibility to obey God.

Make no mistake; God will be glorified in your creation. Either He will be glorified by His righteousness in Christ Jesus toward you, His grace and mercy and lovingkindness displayed in its fullness, creating in us a new heart, bringing us from spiritual death to a new birth, or He will be glorified in the fullness of His righteous wrath and retribution.

But remember your Creator. When He came by the Holy Spirit and made you aware of your lost state in sin. When He gave you a new heart and you believed by faith in the work of the Lord Jesus Christ. Remember the joy you felt and the meaning that life now held for you?

Though I don't know the spiritual condition of those in this room, or those reading this, I trust most of you have been saved from your sins and the wrath to come, and in these twilight years, you are looking forward for that day when the New Jerusalem will come down, and God will wipe away every tear, and there will be no more pain and no more sorrow, and Jesus will be among us, forever and ever, bless the Holy Name.

But, if you are here today, and there is enmity in your heart, I pray that God will save you. For you, there is no bliss, but blight. No resurrection to life eternal, but a reckoning of eternal misery in the fiery pit created for the devil and his angels. If this is your case, cry out to God for Him to save you from your sin. Remember and hear what Peter said in Acts 3:19-23.

"Repent therefore and be converted, that your sins may be blotted out, so that times of refreshing may come from the presence of the Lord, and that He may send Jesus Christ, who was preached to you before, whom heaven must receive until the times of restoration of all things, which God has spoken by the mouth of all His holy prophets since the world began. For Moses truly said to the fathers, 'The Lord you God will raise up for you a Prophet like me from your brethren, Him you shall hear in all things, whatever He says to you. And it shall be that every soul who will not hear that Prophet shall be utterly destroyed from among the people'"

My friends, we cannot keep the commands of God in its totality, though it is our responsibility, but Jesus did, and through faith, His righteousness is imputed unto us. Remember your Creator, and all He has done on our behalf, and let us give Him the glory with all our heart soul and mind.

So let us hear the conclusion of it all.

"FEAR GOD AND KEEP HIS COMMANDS, FOR THAT IS THE WHOLE DUTY OF MAN."

Now may the God and Father of our Lord Jesus Christ bless you and keep you until we meet again. Shalom.

TWO SONS

There was a day when Jesus was teaching in the temple, and being confronted by the chief priests and elders of the people he asked them a question.

"What do you think? A man had two sons. And he went to the first and said 'Son go and work in the vineyard today.' And he answered, 'I will not,' but afterward he changed his mind and went. And he went to the other son and said the same. And he answered, 'I go, sir' but did not go. Which of the two did the will of his father? They said, "The first." Jesus said to them, "Truly, I say to you, the tax collectors and the prostitutes go into the kingdom of God before you."-Matthew 21:28-31 (ESV)

Last time we met, we looked at King Solomon, the wisest and probably the richest man who ever lived, who had a great beginning. He had King David for his father, a man who composed so many wonderful psalms, and while he had his faults, he is known as a man after God's own heart; what a legacy. Just reading Psalm 119 will give you an idea of David's heart, and while we don't have it written for us, there is no reason to think that Solomon was not instructed by his father.

We also have his mother, Bathsheba. Though she committed adultery with King David, which was a tragic event that you can read about later, we mustn't think that she didn't instruct her son in a right way to live. There is no way to be certain of this, but I personally think that Proverbs 31 is the instruction of Bathsheba to her son Solomon. Now is not the time to explore why I think this, and the scripture does say King Lemuel, so we must let scripture be our authority. However, as Solomon is accredited with the authorship of most of the proverbs, it is likely he was aware of this one as well. All speculation aside, Solomon had a great beginning, being visited by God twice, had supremely God given wisdom, and yet ended badly. He remembered his Creator in the days of his youth, but turned away as he got old.

There is another King we are going to look at today who is probably hands down one of the worst, if not the worst, in all of Judah's history. If we add in the northern kingdom of Israel, he is still in contention for the title for the worst of them all, and that is Manasseh, son of King Hezekiah. It is not wrong to think that he probably had a pretty good beginning as well. King Hezekiah was his father and his mother's name was Hephzibah, which means "My delight is in her."

But we also must consider that even though names have significance, that doesn't mean Manasseh's mother taught him about God. Also, at this time in Hezekiah's life he was not necessarily following God like he did when he was younger. I would encourage the reader to go back and read the events in Hezekiah's life found in 2 Kings, 2 Chronicles and Isaiah. So did Manasseh know God in the days of his youth or not? Certainly not in the way Solomon did, but something that has always troubled me, and that is, who were those counselors in Manasseh's youth who so thoroughly turned him against the God of Israel to serve demon idols? Just as an aside, who are you allowing to counsel your children and grandchildren? It is the primary responsibility of parents to teach their children about God and his ways, but we have for the most part, especially here in the United States, abnegated our responsibility to teach them anything. Even in the church we have turned over our children to those who may or may not be qualified to teach them. That is a whole different article in itself, one taught on before, so let's move on.

As mentioned before, Manasseh was a wicked king, just read 2 Kings 21, and it will make you wonder how such a thing could have happened. We also see

God's response here and the devastation pronounced against Judah. But I also want you to read 2 Chronicles 33, especially vss. 10-20. Manasseh repented of all the evil he had done, was restored to the kingship, and did what he could to restore and reform the worship of God which before he had destroyed; he humbled himself greatly. In the end, he remembered the Creator that he knew from his youth.

So how are we to apply this observation into our own lives? For one, it is an encouragement to end well. Everyone to some degree or another knows about God, but not everyone actually KNOWS God. It seems to be that Manasseh knew about God when he was younger, but didn't actually KNOW God until he was much older. And it brings me to that question I am compelled to ask you, do you KNOW God? Is it possible that you have spent your entire life up to this point knowing about God, but not really knowing God. It may seem like a subtle difference, but it really isn't. There are theologians, seminary professors, ministers, elders and deacons in churches all across our land who know about God, and teach about God, even truthfully, but don't KNOW God. So what is the difference you ask? It is manifested primarily in how we live our lives. Those who actually know God, strive to live lives of godliness, doing what is good, while others simply refrain from doing anything bad. Even more importantly though, they have been born again, they have repented of their sin, and tuned back to God with their whole heart. That is why their lives have changed and we can see the difference.

When you look at the end of Manasseh's life, you see much repentance and reform. He was restored to his kingship in Judah and it appears that he spent the last years of his life undoing the idolatry he had established before. He remembered and turned to the God he had learned about in his youth. Yet, it took some really hard life circumstances to get him to that point, but as some of you can attest to, that is sometimes what God uses to get our attention. But our God is also a God of mercy, grace and long-suffering , and it attentive to the prayer of the truly repentant. We do not have the prayer of Manasseh in our bibles, and whether the one which he is reputed to have prayed is real or not we just don't know. You can find articles about it online, but I thought it might be helpful to include it here.

"O Lord, Almighty God of our fathers, Abraham, Isaac, and Jacob, and of their righteous seed; who hast made heaven and earth, with all the ornament thereof; who hast bound the sea by the word of thy commandment; who hast shut up the deep, and sealed it by thy terrible and glorious name; whom all men fear, and tremble before thy power; for the majesty of thy glory cannot be borne, and thine angry threatening toward sinners is importable: but thy merciful promise is unmeasurable and unsearchable; for thou art the most high Lord, of great compassion, longsuffering, very merciful, and repentest of the evils of men. Thou, O Lord, according to thy great goodness hast promised repentance and forgiveness to them that have sinned against thee: and of thine infinite mercies hast appointed repentance unto sinners, that they may be saved. Thou therefore, O Lord, that art the God of the just, hast not appointed repentance to the just, as to Abraham, and Isaac, and Jacob, which have not sinned against thee; but thou hast appointed repentance unto me that am a sinner: for I have sinned above the number of the sands of the sea. My transgressions, O Lord, are multiplied: my transgressions are multiplied, and I am not worthy to behold and see the height of heaven for the multitude of mine iniquities. I am bowed down with many iron bands, that I cannot lift up mine head, neither have any release: for I have provoked thy wrath, and done evil before thee: I did not thy will, neither kept I thy commandments: I have set up abominations, and have multiplied offences. Now therefore I bow the knee of mine heart, beseeching thee of grace. I have sinned, O Lord, I have sinned, and I acknowledge mine iniquities: wherefore, I humbly beseech thee, forgive me, O Lord, forgive me, and destroy me not with mine iniquites. Be not angry with me for ever, by reserving evil for me; neither condemn me to the lower parts of the earth. For thou art the God, even the God of them that repent; and in me thou wilt shew all thy goodness: for thou wilt save me, that am unworthy, according to thy great mercy. Therefore I will praise thee for ever all the days of my life: for all the powers of the heavens do praise thee, and thine is the glory for ever and ever. Amen."

As you can see, it is a very repentant prayer, and whether or not Manasseh actually prayed this prayer, we just don't know. Regardless, it is a prayer similar to those prayers which everyone which goes by the name of "Christian" has prayed. We admitted and confessed our sin before a Holy God, begged Him that in his infinite mercy and grace he would save us, and repented or turned away from sin, and turned to God in faith. Believing what Jesus did on the cross, dying for the guilt and punishment of my sin, that he was buried and three days later rose from the grave, ascended to heaven, and that he is returning to judge those alive and those who are dead. It is by faith in Christ that we are saved, and even that is a gift from God, without which we would never turn to God for repentance in the first place. Also, and we need to know and live this, we have been declared righteous. This righteousness is Jesus' perfect righteousness imputed to us, not our own.

Most of you are familiar with what we call the Sermon on the Mount given by Jesus early in his earthly ministry. It is found in Matthew 5-7, and there are a couple of statements which Jesus makes which is relevant to this article. We need to take seriously everything that the bible teaches us since it is the word of God, but for today look closely at what Jesus teaches us in these two statements. The first is found in chapter 5:20 where he says "For I say to you, that unless your righteousness exceeds the righteousness of the scribes and Pharisees, you will by no means enter the kingdom of heaven."

Pharisees were known for being the most righteous people around. They faithfully kept the sacrifices and Sabbaths, and all the laws which Moses had given, as well as a lot of other ones they had made up. Like Paul says in Romans 10, they had a zeal for God, but not according to knowledge. "For they being ignorant of God's righteousness, and seeking to establish their own righteousness, have not submitted to the righteousness of God."-Romans 10:3 Paul goes on to say in the next verse "For Christ is the end of the law for righteousness to everyone who believes,"

Jesus was declaring that there was a righteousness which went beyond just keeping the law, and he clarifies it throughout the Sermon that pleasing God comes primarily from the heart, not just outward actions. We see this further explained in Romans 3 where we are told that by the deeds of the law, no flesh, meaning any person, will be justified or declared righteous in God's sight. But the righteousness of God apart from the law is through faith in Jesus Christ to all who believe. To somewhat wrap it up, that righteousness which exceeds that of the scribes and Pharisees is God's righteousness imputed to us through faith in Jesus Christ.

The second statement we are going to look at is found in Matt. 7:21-23. "Not everyone who says to Me, 'Lord, Lord,' shall enter the kingdom of heaven, but he who does the will of My Father in heaven. Many shall say to Me in that day, "Lord, Lord, have we not prophesied in Your name, cast out demons in Your name, and done many wonders in Your name?' And then I will declare to them, 'I never knew you; depart from Me you who practice lawlessness."

We see a lot of religious activity done in the name of Jesus, by a lot of people that know about Jesus, but they don't actually KNOW Jesus, and he doesn't know them. It should make everyone ask themselves, especially those who teach and preach the word of God, do I know Jesus and does he know me? In simpler terms, am I saved by faith in Christ? If not, no matter what is happening on the outside, you are practicing lawlessness. Sobering words for those wishing to go into the ministry to think about. So how can we do the will of the Father in heaven and what is it? It is to believe in the one whom He has sent, and that is Jesus.

In reality there are a lot more verses we could look at, and drag this article even further out, but we need to end for today. So we need to ask ourselves what kind of son we are. You are either doing the Father's will or you are not. God has commanded all men and women everywhere to repent, to turn back to him, and have you done so? Not in a superficial way of worship by doing those outward things that you think please God, but from a heartfelt sorrow for the sin which you have committed against Him, clinging and believing in Christ for salvation. Until we truly realize we are sinners, publicans and harlots, we won't see our need for a Savior, and are no better off than those scribes and Pharisees who although they had a form of righteousness, were as out of the will of God as everyone else. Believe in the Lord Jesus Christ and you will be saved, "And this is the will of Him who sent Me, that everyone who sees the Son and believes in Him may have everlasting life; and I will raise him up at the last day."

Hope to see you then, and until next time, Shalom.

THE TRINITY

One of the things about the Christian religion that makes it both loved and hated is its simplicity. When speaking with others about the gospel, we can say such things as Jesus came to save his people from their sin, and whosoever believes in him shall not perish, but have eternal life. That is the good news, that all have sinned, but we have a Savior, if we believe. It seems too easy, and we want to complicate it by trying to add something to it in order to feel like we in some way merited being saved. But then it wouldn't be grace would it. Even our faith or believing is a gift from a Sovereign God, and we have a hard time grasping that sometimes, for again, we want to have a hand in the process. Or we might tell others that Jesus is the only way to the Father, or God, but again some people will hate this statement because it excludes all other religions, the ones that men have made up from the beginning to make themselves feel better. It is simple human nature to think that if I do something good for you, an obligation rests upon you to return the favor. God tells us otherwise.

To be saved, we don't need to know a lot of things such as original sin, the atonement, the Ten Commandments, Old Testament history or even church history, and the list goes on. Yet, the Christian life is enhanced by an understanding of biblical doctrines, for by them we become increasingly aware of who God is, who we are, and what He has done for us.

One such doctrine is that of the trinity, and while we cannot fully comprehend it, to the extent that we can understand, we should do so. Most of us have heard that clique, "Why should we learn doctrine, for doctrine divides?" It should be noted, and always remembers this, that doctrine does NOT divide, it separates. It separates truth from error, and we should be constantly seeking a greater understanding of truth, in order that we might see error for what it is. If those we associate with have no desire for the truth, then perhaps it is time for you to find new companions. That being said, the doctrine of the trinity is easily stated, and we believe it, but not always so easily understood, for in some points it goes beyond the comprehension of our human minds.

Part of the problem lies in the fact that the word "Trinity" is never mentioned in the bible, so what do we mean by saying we believe in the trinity? The simplest definition is that there are three persons which make up what we call the Godhead, that these three persons are the Father, Son, and Holy Spirit. Each one of these persons is fully God, and, there is only ONE God.

Now Christians believe this, but the vast majority of them never give it much thought, and miss out on some of the richness of our salvation. Now each person of the trinity does different things, but it is the same God doing it. For example, the Holy Spirit-God creates in us a new heart in order that we can believe the gospel which says that the Son-God took on human flesh (Jesus), being sent by the Father-God, to live and die and rise again, as a propitiation for our sin, in order that those chosen before the foundation of the world might be saved from their sin, and to demonstrate His great love to all who would believe. It is the ONE God doing all this, but each Person of the trinity having a different part in the process. Yet, because there is a mutual indwelling of the persons of the Trinity, they are all present in every action, for they are ONE God.

So now that you are thoroughly confused (hopefully not), a question which might be running through your mind is, what difference does this make whether or not I know it, can't I just be a disciple of Christ and leave all this to the preachers and teachers, and the seminarians? Of course, but then how do you answer those who say that Jesus was just a created being, the firstborn of all creation? Or that the Holy Spirit is just the power of God, not an actual person? And lastly they may ask, since the trinity isn't mentioned in the bible, how did you make this up?

Something to always remember is that there is no shame in saying I don't know. It is better to have an answer than not, but it does not prove their point if you can't answer them. But it might shake your faith a little bit, which is not good. To be able to say that the bible teaches it, (which it does), and I believe it is commendable, but those asking such questions are deceived, and usually they do not know they have been deceived. It is good to learn those verses which demonstrate that the Holy Spirit is God, such as in Acts 5:1-4 where Ananias is accused of lying to the Holy Spirit, and then moments later told that he has not lied to man, but to God. We could also look to John 1, where speaking about Jesus, it is said that in the beginning was the Word, and the Word was with God, and the Word was God. Then in later verses it says, that the Word became flesh and dwelt among us, and goes on to further prove the divinity of Christ. So we can say that the doctrine of the trinity is a revealed doctrine. But it is good to know these verses in order that we can show them to others.

There are many great books and treatises on the trinity, some of which go into great detail and can be quite hard to follow. But one which I particularly like is from an article "Trinity" by B.B. Warfield. In it he says that the trinity "embodies a truth which has never been discovered, and is indiscoverable, by natural reason." It is something which must be revealed to mankind. "As the doctrine of the Trinity is indiscoverable by reason, so it is incapable of proof from reason." In other words we might say that or must say that God must reveal this idea of the Trinity to us, or it would never be known. And, because our human minds are incapable of fully understanding it, we by faith believe it in so far as God has been pleased to reveal it to us.

For just a moment, as we wrap this up, let's go back to that individual who says that the Son of God was just a created being. If so, what was he? He can't simply be an angel or he would have been declared as so. And being a created being, of course he can't be God, and he can't be a human, for it is declared that the first man created was Adam, so what was the Son of God if he was created? Anyone who seriously thinks about it realizes the dangerous implications of saying that a created being, a finite being, is God. Going back to that verse in John, "In the beginning was the Word, and the Word was with God, and the Word was God"

In a couple of weeks, we are going to return to this topic and look at some more of those verses which declare the divinity of each of the persons of the

Godhead, and a couple of the dangers of incorrectly thinking about the Trinity. In the meantime, there are many systematic books on the internet that have lengthy sections on this very important topic, and if you get a chance, read some of them. Until then, Shalom.

PSALM 119

(Dedicated to sister Katrece)

If you have been a Christian any length of time at all, then you have come across this wonderful psalm, and if for some chance you have not, skip this and read it instead. Surely it will do you more good. We are only going to look at a few minor details concerning this psalm today, but it is my intention that if you have not read or studied it in a while, that you might spend the next several days concentrating on its message.

Most of you are aware that recently I have not been posting as often as before, (originally written early 2019) the reason being I have taken on some other obligations which takes up quite a bit of time. That isn't a total excuse, the other one being my self-discipline in my spare time isn't what it used to be. One of the reasons I mention this is that you might pray I use my time more wisely, but secondarily that we might all think more carefully of how we spend our time. There are some things that are necessities that we spend our time on, such as work and family obligations, but as Christ's disciples, our primary attention should be on the things of God. As Colossians 3 says, we are to set our minds on those things above, (heaven) not on the things of this earth. Our focus is to be on eternal things, not temporal.

So what does any of this have to do with psalm 119? I want to turn your attention for a moment to verse 97, perhaps the key verse of the whole psalm. "Oh how I love your law! It is my meditation all the day." (ESV) This psalm is all about turning our attention back to the eternal and not focusing on that which quickly fades away, the temporal. God is to be on our mind all day long. We meditate on who He is, and what He has done and is doing for us, the salvation He has provided for us in Christ, and what it means to be included as one of "His people". We could easily get caught up here in endless praise, (and why not?), but when we meditate on the law of God, we should understand it encompasses everything. We say "LAW" and immediately most people think of do's and don'ts, and while that is a part of it, I think it much better to say it is to be our way of life.

For a moment let us remember that this is an acrostic psalm, each segment beginning with a different letter of the Hebrew alphabet, and each segment having eight lines, each beginning with that same Hebrew letter. Now throughout this psalm, there are eight different designations that are used for the law of God, though not necessarily in each segment. I don't think it is necessary to take this any further than that, but we will mention these eight designations. There is the law, testimonies, precepts, statutes, commandments, judgements, word, which is sometimes sayings, and lastly, way.

It is the Holy Spirit that has penned these words through the instrumentation of David most likely, but regardless, it is God Himself instructing us in the way of life, the way of blessedness, the way of righteousness, and this psalm goes through the whole range of human experience. As mentioned earlier, we are not going to expound this psalm, but I just wanted to bring it before you afresh that you may spend some time meditating on the riches of its treasury. It is said that we mine the scriptures for those nuggets of wisdom, and to the one who breaks open the psalm aright; there is treasure for a lifetime and beyond. So we will look at the first verse, and then hopefully you will search deeper into the wisdom which God has hidden here.

"Blessed are the undefiled in the way, who walk in the law of the Lord." Blessed, or favored by the Lord, are those who obey Him. We read these words with a little sadness, for originally life was meant to be in full communion and enjoyment in the presence of God. That is where true contentment and fulfillment come from; an obedience to God. I had planned on writing my masters dissertation on "The obedience of faith", but life has a way of changing our plans sometimes, but without obedience, there will be no contentment or fulfillment in the joys of life. The song Trust and Obey is so right. But sometimes our way becomes strewed with obstacles of this life, and our obedience fades, and we let our way become defiled by the temporary pleasures of life, no matter if they are good or bad. Psalm 119 is a good reminder and teacher to lead us back to the paths of righteousness. "How can a young man cleanse his way? By taking heed according to your word." These words taken from verse nine are not only for the young man, but for the old man and the old women, the maiden and the child, and for all who would be godly and set their hearts upon the things of God.

We could go on for quite some time, seeing how long this psalm is, but it would take more time then we have today. I have had the privilege of reading the teachings of Thomas Manton on this psalm, as well as that from Spurgeon's Treasuries of David, and while the insight from the perusal of that material is priceless, it cannot compare to the words of the psalm itself. May we pray for one another that we could just for a moment keep the wonderful way we see enlightened before our eyes in this psalm.

In closing, I want to just spend a brief moment and thank my sister Katrece. She is your sister too, if you are a member of the household of faith, and someday I am confident I will, along with you, meet her again. She reminded me of the precious place this psalm, as well as the rest of the word of God has in our life, and this is my way of thanking her. Thank you Katrece.

Now until we meet again, whether here in the pages of this blog, or in the realm of eternity, may God bless you. Shalom.

STREET EPISTEMOLOGY AND FAITH (ONCE I WAS BLIND BUT NOW I SEE)

If someone were to ask you why you believe that there is a God or Creator, and why the God of the Bible is the one and only true God, how would you answer that? Now we are not going to address that question specifically today, but we will spend a few moments and talk about faith.

Most of you do not know what street epistemology is, or even what epistemology is, and I must admit I had never heard of street epistemology until Sky mentioned it on a comment on my last post. Thank you Sky, and I truly mean that. If you do not know what epistemology is, this is one of those times where I am going to force you to look it up in your dictionary, or to be more modern, online. Now street epistemology is an interesting concept, and while I don't necessarily agree with the reason it is being done, it is an effective tool in forcing people to confront their beliefs. Why do you believe what you believe; and this is a most appropriate question.

 For those of you who read these posts, thank you. Hopefully they are enriching your life, but if not, at least I hope you find them entertaining. But most importantly, they are designed to make you think. To think about what it means to be a Christian, and how you are to live your life, and to give those who are not Christians, a view or proclamation of the gospel.

Now in its simplest terms, the gospel is that good news that Jesus came to save sinners, that all men are sinners, and that those who believe or have faith in Christ, will not perish, but have eternal life. That he has come to save them from the wrath of God against all who sin, and that wrath is eternal damnation and torment in what we call hell. But why do you believe? Is this not a fair question to ask yourself?

We evangelize, or proclaim this gospel, because we know it to be true, but why do you know it to be true? In some ways, this is the easiest question to answer, but at the same time it is not palatable to those with whom we speak, and why is that? It is because faith comes by hearing, and hearing by the word of

God. Which brings us to the big question we are attempting to address here, and that is, what is faith?

We have a definition of it in Hebrews 11:1 which says, "Now faith is the substance of things hoped for, the evidence of things not seen." This is a very good and sufficient definition for some, but it is perhaps for the non-Christian, somewhat vague or even nonsensical. So how do we define faith in a way which all may understand?

Now in those classes of systematic theology which I took, faith plays an important part, but it is difficult at times to explain in a post, what it took a week and a half of material to go over. And even in that week and a half, there was not sufficient time to go over all the details. So how do we define faith quickly and succinctly; not easily that is for sure? So though our examples may be somewhat simplistic, we ask the reader to be thoughtful and consider the truths.

Now most of us have not been to China, but we have faith that it is there, we believe that it is there. We base this on evidence of people who have been there and have actually seen it. The evidence is overwhelming, and we never even give it a second thought, though we have never been there. By faith we understand it to be, through the evidence of testimony.

By faith, we believe that the sun will rise in the east in the morning. Let us not get into semantics, for we all know that the sun is basically stationary, and given that clouds might obstruct our view, etc. but the sun will come up in the morning. And how do you know that? Not only do we have the testimony of history, but we know it to be so of our own experience.

We know that man has been to the moon, (at least most of us do) based on testimony of a few individuals. I haven't been to the moon and except for a few rocks which supposedly came from the moon, I have no proof that man has been to the moon, except as mentioned before, from reliable testimony.

Now as stated earlier, we cannot go into explicit detail, but when it comes to the Christian faith, we believe it on the testimony of God, as revealed in His scriptures, the bible. To quote Charles Hodge here, "The fulfillment of prophecies, the miracles of its authors (bible) its contents and the effects which it produces are rational grounds to believe it is from God...."the proximate end of these manifestations of supernatural foresight was to authenticate the divine mission of the messengers of God. And the people were called upon to receive their message and to believe on the authority of God, by whom they were sent."

We can have no other foundation to base our faith on than the testimony of God. Part of the problem of explaining faith, or why we believe to others, is we do not realize that this evidence, the testimony of God, is sufficient and we need no other. What some theologians or philosophers have done, is try to explain faith in either a philosophical way, or in a rational way, or sometimes one based on feelings, instead of the truths of God's own testimony. Additionally, there are some questions concerning God which our minds are not capable of understanding, yet rationalists assume that we must be able to answer them, and they cannot be answered. When men have tried, they have gone into areas of useless and futile speculation and/or great levels of heretical teachings. Not all truths can be known through reasoning, but simple taken on authority.

Now given this, there are three types of faith we commonly see in the church, and that is speculative faith, temporary faith, and saving faith. Now those having speculative faith, or even temporary faith, for the most part believe everything we stated before, that the scriptures are the words and revelation which God has given to us, and that they are true. The moral obligations and the truths revealed to the consciousness and mind they have no doubt as to why they believe, but it is all external. It reminds us of what it says in James, that even the demons believe and tremble. They know it to be true and have great fear as there is no salvation on their behalf, but only a constant dread of what awaits them in the future.

But saving faith, that faith which comes from a regenerated heart is not based solely on external and moral evidences, but from a supernatural work of the Holy Spirit, which by an inward experience causes us to believe the testimony and authority of God. This faith based on the inward testimony of the Spirit is that new birth, a new creation, and what the spirit reveals to us, we know to be true.

This faith also manifests itself in a changed life, slowly in some, faster in others. This type of faith seems strange to some, for it is a new creation, taking a spiritually dead soul and making it alive, which is something only God can do.

"Now the natural man does not receive the things of the Spirit of God, for they are foolishness to him; nor can he know them, because they are spiritually discerned."-1 Corinthians 2:14

Now when someone asks us why we believe or have faith, it isn't always easy to give an answer which they find satisfactory. But the point is, we are best off when we explain what we believe and that we believe it on the testimony of God, which he has authenticated by an inward work in our heart by the Holy Spirit. We have been changed, regenerated, born again, and that is not always explainable because it is spiritually discerned. As it says, the Spirit testifies to our spirit of the things of God.

While all of this is good to know, most of us don't know how to explain it in this way, but we shouldn't be discouraged. If they are honestly and sincerely asking why we believe what we do, struggling to explain won't be a problem, but if they are antagonistic or have ulterior motives, no answer will be sufficient.

But if you think about it, and be encouraged by this, one of the best answers ever given was simply I don't know how all this works, except to say once I was blind, but now I see. Until next time, Shalom.

THE DEITY OF THE SON OF GOD

Every few weeks ago we post a short article on some aspect of systematic theology, and the last one we did was on the trinity. At that time we gave a simple definition, and that was that there are three persons which make up what we call the Godhead. These three persons are the Father, the Son, and the Holy Spirit. Each one of these persons are fully God, nevertheless, there is only ONE God. We are continuing today by looking at the deity of one of these persons, and that is the Son of God, Jesus Christ.

It isn't as hard for our minds to grasp that the Father is God, or we say God the Father, and unbelievers reading this are used to that concept that God is the Father of us all. But we will mention a couple of verses in passing for everyone to look at. By the way, and it has been said before, but when we say unbeliever, we are speaking about those who have not yet trusted Jesus as their Savior, not atheists. Perhaps next time we shall look at atheism so called, and practical atheism, but for now, let us look at the God and Father of our Lord Jesus Christ.

First Peter 1:2 speaks of God the Father, as well as Jude 1, and there are others, but perhaps one of the best passages is from the lips of Jesus Himself in John 20:17. Mary Magdalene had gone to the tomb of Jesus, and finding it empty went to Peter and (John) informing them that Jesus was no longer there. They all went back to the tomb and when they saw it was empty, the disciples went back to their homes, but Mary remained. It is a beautiful story we have here, but Jesus revealing Himself to Mary tells her to go and say to His brothers, "I am ascending to my Father and your Father, to my God and your God." This is a marvelously profound statement when we realize that the Father and God of our Lord and Savior Jesus Christ, is our God and Father, and, that Jesus is that God. Our minds can scarcely grasp this, and in its totality we cannot.

"In the beginning was the Word, and the Word was with God, and the Word was God."-John 1:1

"He was in the beginning with God."-John 1:2

"And the Word became flesh and dwelt among us. And we have seen His glory, glory as the Son from the Father, full of grace and truth."-John 1:14 (ESV)

How can we not break out into doxology here? We have said it before, and probably will again, but look at some of the Apostle Paul's doxologies. Anytime he started writing and contemplating on the wonders of the grace and love that God has shown us in the face of Jesus Christ, he couldn't contain himself, and neither should we. This is not the only instance, but each one of us could with Paul shout out this doxology, "But I received mercy for this reason, that in me, as the foremost, Jesus Christ might display his perfect patience as an example to those who were to believe in Him for eternal life. To the King of the ages, immortal, invisible, the only God, be honor and glory forever and ever. Amen."-1Timothy 1:16-17 (ESV)

There is nothing in us that is commendable, yet God to the praise of His glorious grace has chosen us IN CHRIST to spend eternity in an intimate union with Himself; in the presence and communion of His glory. And God is this Christ, who as the Son of God came that whosoever believed in Him might have eternal life and not perish.

Have we not rambled on somewhat here? There are so many different passages we could look at concerning the deity of Christ that it's hard to pick just a few, but John 8:58 is a good place to start. Jesus is speaking to the Jews, and it would be good if you read the whole chapter, but they are speaking about Abraham and Jesus tells them "Your father Abraham rejoiced that he would see my day. He saw it and was glad." The Jews then ask if he had seen Abraham, at which point Jesus answered and said, "Truly, Truly, I say to you, before Abraham was, I AM." At which point they picked up stones to throw at him, because they thought he had committed blasphemy by equating himself as God.

Several passages in the book of Revelation are worthwhile to look at, but Rev. 22:12-16 seems to make it clear, Jesus is LORD and God. He is the Alpha and Omega, the first and the last, the beginning and the end.-v.13.

We haven't even looked at the miracles that Jesus performed. Healing the sick, raising the dead, causing the blind to see, turning water to wine, and John says at the end of his gospel, that Jesus did so many things that if they were all written down, the world couldn't contain the books that would be written. But John ends chapter 20 with a statement that truly tells it all, that what we do have written for us is in order that we may believe that Jesus is the Christ, the Son of God, and that believing you may have life in His name.

For the most part we try and keep these posts from being too long and since there are a couple of more things to consider, we will continue in a couple of days. In the meantime, we have to ask, have you believed in Jesus for salvation? There is such a great passage in John chapter 3 where Jesus is speaking to Nicodemus, and tells him that unless one is born again, they cannot see the Kingdom of God. Then a little bit later we have that famous verse 3:16, and in closing today, v.18. "Whoever believes in him is not condemned, but whoever does not believe is condemned already, because he has not believed in the name of the only Son of God." (ESV)

If you are reading this and have not yet believed, what are you waiting for? You are under a sentence of condemnation, and today is the day of salvation. Today may be your last, and as we have mentioned before, it is appointed for all to die, and then the judgement. We plead with you, be reconciled to God.

Until next time, Shalom.

BEING IN THE FORM OF GOD

Today we are going to continue looking at the life of Jesus and some aspects concerning His deity which we often overlook. We will start by reading some verses from the Apostle Paul's letter to the Philippians. In chapter 2, beginning in verse 3 we have this exhortation on how to act towards others.

"Let nothing be done through selfish ambition or conceit, (pride) but in lowliness of mind (humility) let each esteem others better than himself. Let each of you look out not only for his own interests, but also for the interests of others."

Paul is writing to these Christians, as well as to us, to be unified by their love for one another, and this can only happen when we humble ourselves and lookout for the well-being of others. Now it is not in our nature to be humble, much less look out for the interests of others, unless of course it is in OUR best interest to do so, so Paul encourages us by reminding us of Jesus, to be like minded.

"Let this mind be in you which was also in Christ Jesus, who being in the form of God, did not count equality with God a thing to be grasped, (held on to) but emptied Himself by taking the form of a servant (slave) and coming in the likeness of man. And being found in appearance as a man, He humbled Himself and became obedient to the point of death, even the death of the cross."- Philippians 2:5-8

When we think about Jesus, or read about Jesus, it should never stray out of our minds, that He is God. In our everyday speech, it is easy to slip and say something like "He Was God", or to think of Him as the Son of God, but not fully God. Even though we know better, it is our tendency to think of Jesus, the son of God, and the Holy Spirit as somewhat lesser beings than God. But they are not lesser beings, and Christ being in the "Form of God", never ceased from being fully God. Yet, knowing He was fully God, with all those incommunicable and communicable attributes we read of in scripture, He chose to live a life like a man. "But when the fullness of the time had come, God sent forth His Son, born of a woman, born under the law, to redeem those who were under the law, that we might receive the adoption as sons."-Galatians 4:4-5

When we read "Being in the form of God", it seems pretty easy to understand, but just to be clear we'll look at it more closely. The word that we translate as being has the idea of originality. Originally, Christ was (Is) in the form of God, and the word used for form means everything associated with that thing that makes it what it is. And what we are looking at is God. So we might be able to say that originally, Christ Jesus was fully God, but at the incarnation, He took on the "Form" of a bondservant or slave; Christ became everything that makes up being a bondservant or slave. "And being found in appearance (Fashion) as a man", simply means that in His earthly existence his outward appearance was as a man. There was nothing outwardly that distinguished him from any other man. But being made or coming in the "Likeness of men" implies not simply that outward appearance, but a human nature.

We must be careful here that we don't fall into that error of thinking that it was in appearance only, and the Son of God wasn't really human. What makes us human is having a body and a soul; that is our nature. And as it says in John 1, the Word (God) became flesh, and dwelt among us. God the Son took upon Himself a human nature, (Body and soul), and by doing so became One person with two natures. As the Son of God, His being was in the form of God, this Person of the Trinity, whose nature was God, came into the world in the likeness of men, having a body and soul, in order to take on a human nature. So what we have is One Person with two natures. These natures are not mixed so as to make one combined nature, but remain separate, so Christ Jesus was fully God, and fully human, yet without sin. Just as in the Trinity we have three persons with One nature, (God) and we cannot fully comprehend it, so it is here. One person with two separate natures is not fully explainable either.

However, in 451 A.D., the Council of Chalcedon, in order to make a clear statement regarding what scripture teaches about our Lord Jesus Christ, came up with this formula which incorporates it all.

Jesus Christ our Lord is "truly God and truly man, of a reasonable soul and body; consubstantial with the Father according to the Godhead, and consubstantial with us according to the manhood; in all things like unto us, without sin; begotten before all ages of the Father according to the Godhead, and in these latter days, for us and for our salvation, born of the Virgin Mary, the Mother of God, according to the manhood; one and the same Christ, Son, Lord, Only-begotten, to be acknowledged in two natures inconfusedly, inchangeably, indivisibly, inseparably; the distinction of natures being by no means taken away by the union, but rather the property of each nature being preserved, and concurring in one Person and one subsistence, not parted or divided into two persons, but one and the same Son, and Only-begotten, God the Word, the Lord Jesus Christ."

Now with all that being said, you might be asking what is the point in all of this, couldn't you have said all that in a much simpler way? Probably, but I'm not that skilled. What we need to ask ourselves after seeing what all has transpired in the incarnation of the Son of God, is why? Why in the world would God want to condescend or humble Himself and take on human flesh? The simple answer is for our salvation, and because of the love, grace and mercy of God. "For God so loved the world that He gave His only begotten Son, that whosoever believed on Him might not perish, but have eternal life."-John 3:16 "But God demonstrates His own love for us, in that while we were still sinners, Christ died for us."-Romans 5:8 Later read Ephesians 2:1-10 for another reason, but we might sum it all up and say that it is all to the praise of His glorious grace.

This is what Paul is getting at when he tells us to do nothing from selfish ambition or conceit, but that we are to humble ourselves and count others as more significant and worthy than us. That as we look out for our own interest, be especially looking out for the interests of others. And then, Paul gives us the example of God in Christ doing that for us. Think about it for a minute, what if God was not looking out for our best interest? And on top of that, as rebellious sinners at enmity against Him, why should He even look out for our best interest?

We need to be more conscious about this in our dealings with others. Do you see what God did? He became our servant, doing those things which were in our best interest, yet at no time did He not realize that He was God. During His life on earth, how many people do you think Jesus healed that never believed in a saving way? And knowing that they would not believe, He healed them anyway. Shouldn't we do likewise and look out for the interests of others, considering them worthy and significant of our servanthood, while knowing who they really are? We could come up with numerous examples, but each one of us should examine our own life and see those people who we are to serve, and then serve them. Our pride says no, we are better than them, they should serve us. But as we close, and hopefully this has been helpful in some way, remember this always, that God, the Son, being found in human form, He HUMBLED Himself, for us, and we should do the same for others, deserving or not.

Think on these things, and until we meet again, Shalom.

FERVENCY IN PRAYER

"The effectual fervent prayer of a righteous man availeth much."- James 5:16

For those of you who grew up in a church environment, this was probably among the first verses that you memorized. Take a moment and reflect on those early years and see if you remember those familiar verses, Genesis 1:1, John 3:16, and the 23rd Psalm. There are others of course, and as we grow older there are others we put into our memory banks, but the ones we learn when we are young seem to always stick, and James 5:16 is one of them.

Personally, I have always liked the books of Genesis and Revelation, because it tells us the beginning of all things and the end, and for some reason or another I find that comforting. Now I am not going to say that Genesis 1:1 is my favorite verse, (it might be) but it is probably the most important verse in the entire Bible. I know that is a strong statement and others might disagree, but the point being is that most of us learn this verse when we are young, and tend to never consider all that is said in those few words. And so it is in the verse we are glancing at today. We read it, we memorize it, but do we consider how it relates to our personal prayer life? Are your prayers effectual, and do they avail? More importantly, are you praying fervently, and what does that mean? Let us spend a few minutes looking at this and see if we might get some insight into it.

It is unfortunate that some of our versions of the Bible don't have the word fervent in it, and admittedly that word is not used directly in the Greek, but it is intimated, and personally I think we suffer in the meaning of the verse if we don't use it. You can look all that up if you want to, but fervency is quite appropriate and keeps with the meaning of the passage. Regardless, there should be a sense of fervency or passionate intensity in all our prayers to God. After all, if you aren't serious about it, why should God be? I think all of us could say that too often we approach God in prayer as a duty, rather than a privilege. Everything we do should have the glory of God in mind, including our prayers and the content of our prayers, but is that what you are doing when you approach God in prayer?

Now we are not going to dissect every aspect of this verse, because it would take too much time, or space, but we are assuming that the individual who is fervent in prayer, is a righteous person, one who would profess to be a Christian. And as a Christian, we desire that the will of God be done, on earth as it is in heaven, though in many instances we do not know what that is. It could be that a loved one is sick and dying of the covid virus and we pray "fervently" that they be healed, yet it could be God's will that this is the means by which their life will be ended. Even when we pray fervently, it doesn't mean we get the answer we desire, but, if the glory of God is our greatest concern, then the answer we get is the one which avails much; we are pleased with the answer.

And yet is it not true that many if not most of our prayers are self-serving? We ask the Lord for our daily bread, and in many if not most cases He provides not only our daily needs, but much more besides, and yet do we use that extra for the benefit of the Kingdom and others, or for ourselves? We tithe our stimulus check and then go out and buy a $1000 barbeque grill. (Just in case anyone wonders, I did not buy a grill, just an example) This is always something that is between you and the Lord, so we cannot guilt one another in these areas, but it is something to think about. When we ask for the forgiveness of sin, is it to ease the conscience and the consequences, or that the glory of God's grace in our repentance may be displayed? We who call ourselves teachers or preachers, do we ask that our words glorify God in vain, because in fact it is our own pride and glory we are concerned about? Each individual must contemplate this alone, begging that God would show them their heart in this matter, for our hearts are deceitful and full of wickedness.

Now admittedly, we have gotten somewhat off topic, and that is fervent prayer, so let us look at a few examples of fervent prayer and how they were answered. For time's sake we will not get into a lot of detail on each one, but go and read them later and meditate on how they might be useful in edification. There are many more examples in scripture then the ones here, especially in the psalms, but in each case, ask yourself how God was glorified in each answer, and whether or not the petitioner got the answer they were seeking?

The first one is when Abraham was petitioning the Lord concerning the destruction of Sodom. We find the story in Genesis 18:16-33, and you can read the event for yourself, but v. 25 is key; "Shall not the Judge of all the earth do right?" Though surely Abraham was concerned about his nephew Lot, wasn't he also concerned that the Judge of all the earth might err in destroying the righteous along with the wicked and the name of God be impugned? The second is found in Samuel 1:10-18. Hannah was in bitterness of soul and wept in anguish as she prayed to the Lord. She was pouring out her soul to the Lord, and as you read the story, you can almost feel the intensity or fervency in which she prayed. All she wanted was a son, but even then she was willing to give him back to the Lord, and she did, and just listen to her prayer of thanksgiving in the beginning of chapter 2. It is just a few short verses, but look at all that it contains. Next we look at Paul. The apostle Paul was a great man of prayer, and intensely dedicated to the glorifying of God, but I sometimes think that some of the most fervent prayers he ever prayed were the ones concerning the thorn in his flesh. Three times he pleaded with the Lord that it might be removed, but what was the answer? The Lord answers Paul and says "My grace is sufficient for you, for My strength is made perfect in weakness." No matter what happens in our life, is not the grace of God sufficient for us? And lastly, let us look at the fervent prayer of our Lord Himself, Jesus in the garden of Gethsemane. In Matthew 26:36-46, we read that Jesus asks the Father three times that if it is possible that "this cup" which He was to drink concerning all the events that were to shortly come to pass, might be taken from Him. Yet, Jesus also says, "nevertheless, not as I will, but as You will." In Luke's telling of this event we read that Jesus was in agony and prayed more earnestly or fervently, and His sweat became like great drops of blood falling to the ground. For our sake He endured the cross.

When we look at these examples and others in the Bible, we see an intensity with which people prayed, and a not letting go until God answered their prayer. And in those instances where the answer seemed to be a NO, yet the will and glory of God and His sovereignty was sufficient. What is it like for you? Is your morning prayer forgotten before you even finish your coffee? Many people make prayer lists; I have done so myself, but ask yourself why you made the list in the first place? Now we can come boldly before the throne of God, but reverently, and are you coming with bold petitions? It could be that prayers of thanksgiving are all that are necessary at the moment, but are you doing it earnestly, fervently? Now much more could and can and should be said on this topic, but we will close with a quote from John Owen taken somewhat out of context, but appropriate for what we are looking at. Hopefully this gives you something to think about for today, and until we meet next, Shalom

"There is no duty which is in this world we perform unto God that is more acceptable unto Him than fervent prayers for a right understanding of his mind and will in his word; for hereon all the glory we give unto him, and the due performance of all our obedience do depend."

LESSONS FROM PINBALL

"When I was a child, I spoke as a child, I understood as a child, I thought as a child; but when I became a man, I put away childish things."-1 Corinthians 13:11

Ever since I was a young boy I played the silver ball...does anyone out there remember or know what I am referring to? For those of us who might be a little older, and especially those of us who were pinball aficionados or fanatics, these words are very familiar. Now I understand that the computer video games of today are much more addicting than the games of pinball we used to play, but I bet there are many of us who could admit to spending hours in the pool hall or bowling alley playing our favorite game. There was even a broken down six story hotel that had a couple of games in their lobby that me and a couple of friends used to haunt. But those days are over, or are they?

The verse we are looking at today is going to be taken somewhat out of context, for it is referencing more of a spiritual attitude, much like we see in Hebrews 5:12-6:3. There is a time to partake of spiritual milk, and there is a time to move on to solid food. We are to progress in spiritual maturity and sanctification until that day we reach perfection, which won't happen in this lifetime, but have we put away childish things? And, what are childish things when it comes to the Christian life? Again looking at Hebrews we begin to get an answer and that it is those foundational things that are necessary. Just as a child must have a foundational understanding of the alphabet in order to mature into reading and writing, so there are foundational things we learn when we first become Christians. But at a certain point we move on. I seriously doubt if there is anyone reading this who practices his or her abc's every day, but how many of us are no further along in our Christian maturity then we were say ten or twenty years ago? Or perhaps you have increased in faith but you know others who haven't; why is this? It could be that you or they are as it says in Hebrews 6:12, sluggish or just lazy. Or maybe you haven't put away the childish things of this world.

There comes a day when you put the pinball machine away. That doesn't mean there is anything wrong with playing pinball or other games for that matter, but it is time to be mature. We have more important things that need to be done. I think you understand that we aren't saying recreation is wrong, for you could substitute pinball with whatever might be your particular form of distraction. For some it is an inordinate amount of time spent watching television, or listening to the radio, or attending sports functions, being on the computer, maybe even working too much. We could enlarge the list, but the fact of the matter is there is always something that can keep our minds off of the things of God and leave us in a childlike state. But we are no longer children are we? So if this describes you, why are you continuing to indulge in childish things, when you have attained a state of maturity? Each of us probably knows individuals who have never graduated high school. What I mean by that is that they finished school, but they live their life as if they were still in high school. If you do know someone like this you realize how pathetic it can be at times.

Now there are many ways we could branch off from here, and into useful ways as well, but wanted to keep it short and simple this week, so let us close by asking if we might be holding onto pathetic and childish ways concerning our Christian walk. Are you refusing to let go of some pet sin? You may have convinced yourself it is a small thing, but can we really actually call any sin small? Was it not a little sin that put our Savior on the cross; the eating of a piece of fruit? Are we holding onto some man made doctrine rather than biblical doctrine that is causing division? There are a lot of those aren't there. Are we neglecting some of our Christian duties in order that we might ...fill in the blank, because it is more fun or easier? The Christian life isn't always easy if we intend to walk increasingly more Christ like and become mature.

It is time to put away childish things. Until next time, Shalom

PSALM 103:1-5

Just to let the reader know, this was originally written in that period of time after we had been banned by Facebook, and were sending out these short notes by e-mail. There weren't that many people we were sending it out to, and it was very discouraging that there was virtually no response, positive or negative. But the Lord has a way of encouraging us even in those dark days of depression.

"Bless the Lord, O my soul, and all that is within me, bless his holy name! Bless the Lord, O my soul, and forget not all his benefits, who forgives all your iniquity, who heals all your diseases, who redeems your life from the pit, who crowns you with steadfast love and mercy, who satisfies you with good so your youth is renewed like the eagle's." Ps. 103:1-5 (ESV)

Oh what a peace, that Shalom from God that comforted me in this time.

There is something striking here that we seldom take into account, or perhaps have never thought about, and that is the necessity to remind our soul to remember all the benefits that God has bestowed upon us. It is the mind telling the soul to remember what the Lord has done. Now the psalms are songs of poetry, and we could easily say that nothing more is going on here than the psalmist poetically reminding us to count our many blessings, but when is the last time you talked to your soul? Can we differentiate our mind from our soul? We can get into some deep psychological, philosophical and theological questions here, and it is not our intent to discuss all of that at the moment, but just some simple surface observations.

I believe it was Louis Berkhof who said that "the body is the fit instrument for the self-expression of the soul." But how often do we reflect on that? That when we sing praises or blessings, it is our soul expressing itself physically? Everything that we do, whether good or bad or indifferent, is the soul expressing itself by means of the body. We see Jesus saying basically the same thing in

Matthew 15 when he says that out of the heart comes evil thoughts, etc. and it is these that defile a man; that which comes out of the mouth. So it is the sinning soul which causes the body to manifest that sin, but DO NOT misunderstand: the body is not off the hook, it is guilty of sin also. I think everyone to whom we are writing understands this, but great and grave errors have been committed in the past, and the present for that matter, by individuals who would separate the two (body and soul) for their own nefarious means. The soul and body are ONE and will be united for all eternity, save for that time between death and the resurrection of the body. But, we are wandering off into other areas that though important, are not our focus so back to our psalm.

The Christian, the disciple of Jesus, those to whom we are primarily writing to, have been regenerated, and have been declared righteous and sanctified, and have been adopted into the family and kingdom of God. Now while we live on this earth, our outward appearance of sanctification and righteousness is not always seen by others to the extent it should, but a lot of that is because we do not remind ourselves or our soul, what has happened. And, it is much easier to care and love our neighbor when we remember what has been done for us. The words of Jesus in Matthew 6:14-15 should never be far from our hearts.

"For if you forgive others their trespasses, your heavenly Father will also forgive you, but if you do not forgive others their trespasses, neither will your Father forgive your trespasses." (ESV)

We have been forgiven much, is it so hard to forgive others little? It is a whole lot easier said than done, yet when we daily remember that all our iniquities have been forgiven, it becomes less difficult. When was the last time you contemplated the mass of iniquities you have accumulated in your life and possibly continue to accumulate and then realize they have all been forgiven. Those secret sins which lurk in your heart, which will never outwardly be manifested, are sins nonetheless, and they have been forgiven, and at what cost? One of the benefits of our participation in the Lords Supper is that we are reminded of the cost of the forgiveness of our iniquities. From Isaiah 53 we read that he (speaking of Jesus) was pierced for our transgressions and was crushed for our iniquities and it was the will of the Lord to crush him. And to what purpose was all this? It was so that all our iniquities could be forgiven, because the penalty for them had been paid.

Our life has been redeemed from the pit, or destruction. And for what reason has God chosen you or me or anyone else to so great a salvation? It is to the praise of the glory of His grace. What a wonderful sentence that is, and humbling too. There is nothing special about us, but while we were yet sinners and at enmity to God, he reconciled us to himself through Christ. Most of you know this, or should, but it is by grace you have been saved from destruction. Spend a few minutes and contemplate this great grace which has saved you. Approximately 150,000 people die on a daily basis, and how many of them will go into an eternity of destruction? Yet you have been spared.

We could spend more time on these few verses, especially on how God crowns us with his steadfast love and mercy, but the point today is to remember. To tell your soul not to forget all God's benefits which He has bestowed upon us, individually, as well as corporately as the saints of the living God. And after spending some time meditating on this, I believe you will find that it is time to stand with the psalmist and sing: Bless the Lord O my soul and all that is within me, bless His holy name!

Until next time, Shalom.

OUR CONFRONTATION WITH GOD or THE BLESSING OF CHASTISEMENT

2 Samuel 12:1-7a "You are the man."

If anyone has been a Christian for any length of time, they are most likely aware of Psalm 51. In fact, there are many who could claim that it was this psalm which God used as a means to bring them to faith in Christ; our salvation. It is arguably the greatest (if we can use that word) of the seven penitential psalms, and expresses the full range of confession, repentance and the desire for restoration or reconciliation with God. And though it is a psalm, it is also a prayer, a prayer of lament and grief and sorrow. It is a prayer of a man who cannot look upwards, but beats his breast and cries "Lord, be merciful to me a sinner."

However, this psalm is also the fruit or result of a man who has been confronted by God, and to be confronted by God is not a thing to be taken lightly, though as we will see later, most do. But in order to fully appreciate the degree of sorrow and grief which the psalmist displays in these few verses, we need to know the context behind them. Our text today actually begins in chapter 11 of 1Samuel, and it tells the story of King David of Israel and his adultery with Bathsheba and the ensuing murder of the women's husband, Uriah. And the last two verses of chap.11 tell us much. First of all, when Bathsheba heard that her husband had died, she mourned for him, and when the days of her mourning were over, which was typically seven days, David sent for her and she became his wife and bore him a son.

Now before we read the last sentence of chap. 11, there are some observations and questions that we should consider. First of all, there is no indication that Bathsheba knew that King David had conspired to have her husband killed, or that she ever found out. But at some point in the history of Israel, this event became known, as we have it in our hands today. For that matter it is not certain that the people living at the time were aware of anything unusual, except of course those who were involved in the deeds. Since it is unclear of who the actual author of 2 Samuel was, whether Nathan the prophet or Gad the seer, or someone else even, it is clear that the Holy Spirit deemed it profitable for us to know the details. Personally I like to think that Nathan wrote this part after the death of David, but whether anything was public knowledge before the death of David it is hard to say.

However in psalm 51 it is clearly stated at the beginning, "To the chief musician. A Psalm of David when Nathan the prophet went to him after he had gone in to Bathsheba." And in 2 Sam. 12:14 it states that "Because of this deed you have given great occasion to the enemies of the Lord to blaspheme." These two passages seem to indicate that it was perhaps known to more than just the handful of people involved, but regardless, it is definitely well known now.

(Just as an aside, even today we have leaders who commit atrocities who seemingly are not held accountable in this physical world. Also with the internet and other media outlets their deeds are quickly published and yet it seems to make no difference. In David's case it could have become very well known what he had done but because he was King there were no immediate repercussions as far as the common everyday man could see.)

Nevertheless, we see in the last sentence of chap.11 what really concerns us and that is that "the thing that David had done displeased the Lord." It was an evil in the sight of the Lord, which could not be overlooked; there were to be evil consequences. Why does man think he can hide from the omnipresence and omniscience of God? We read in Psalm 139, another Psalm of David, that no one can flee from the presence of God. (Read v.7-12) Do we really think that the One who inhabits eternity, the One who knows all things that are to come to pass, that knew these before the foundation of the earth, cannot see our deeds? This God knows our thoughts before they even come to pass, and do you think you are then going to be able to hide the manifestations of your many evil thoughts from His eyes? The thought alone is sin, compounded by the actual deed. As Jesus said, whoever looks at a woman to lust for her has already committed adultery with her in his heart. Even the darkness cannot hide you; it is as light before the Lord.

But just for a moment, replace David's name with yours. The thing that you have done has displeased the Lord as well as the thing I have done has displeased the Lord, for all have sinned and come short of the glory of God. What you have done in the dark when no one can see has an open audience before God, possibly even the elect angels as well as the evil ones, the demons. Certainly your thoughts are before God and I think we would all agree that it is good that no one else knows them, yet we would do well to always remember they are ever before Him who is our Judge; sobering thoughts indeed. But again, how often do we act like the atheist and sin presumptuously and willfully against God as if He does not exist? Or, because judgement is not speedily executed, do we think that God has overlooked it? We become comfortable that our sin is hidden and we forget it; it is in our thoughts as if it had never happened; THEN.

What a mighty word THEN is. After we have become comfortable, after we have become complacent, after we have forgotten, THEN God confronts us. And make no mistake; at one time or another God will confront every one of us. Some of you reading or listening to this know exactly what I mean, for you have been confronted by God already. Perhaps it was only in your conscience, and did you listen? Maybe you think in your heart that if God sent a person to confront you directly as Nathan did David, you would listen, but isn't that what your minister does every time he climbs into the pulpit? Is he not declaring that the wages of sin is death and that you are the man? Have you stopped up your ears from listening to what this ambassador from God has to tell you? If this describes you, then you still have that heart of stone you were born with, but may it never be said that God did not confront you.

So what is God's purpose in confronting us? For one thing it is to remind us that God is fully aware of what you have done. As stated earlier, nothing can be hidden from the eyes of the omnipresent God. Another reason is that we understand that there will be consequences for our sin, even for the regenerate. It is true the sins of the regenerate have been forgiven by the blood of Christ, but there will be consequences of some sort in this life. We could come up with all types of examples which are obvious, such as the drunkard who drinks and drives and gets into an accident and harms someone. Prison and monetary consequences are just two considerations, not counting possible health issues or relationship issues which might incur. But often times our sin doesn't have such obvious consequences as our example, and unless God confronts us, our hard hearts dismiss it as a thing not to be concerned about. Yet in one way or another God is continuously confronting us, if we would but listen. The greatest way He does this is by death. How many of us have heard that age old question, "But why did they have to die?" We tend to think that this is just a question that children ask, but it can be heard on the lips of adults just as frequently. And if we do not give them the answer that by one man sin entered into the world and death by sin, because of disobedience to God's command, we have neglected our duty.

Another reason for God confronting us is in order that we might be aware that sometimes, if not all the time, our evil deeds give great occasions to the enemies of the Lord to blaspheme. And we should look at this in two ways. First, those people around us who know we are Christians, see what we do and instinctively know we are playing the hypocrite, if even for a moment. Of course we know that in this life we will continue to sin, but even so, it gives those around us a reason to scorn our Savior. Also, the greater the sin, and the more public the person, the greater damage it does to the profession that we make and to the name by which we are called. We see this on a more regular basis today, where some leader in the church falls into some type of immorality which discredits all he stands for and has taught. This doesn't mean what he taught wasn't true, but it gives great occasion for derision by the enemies of the Lord.

But there is a second way we can look at this, and it is by realizing that there is a great host of spiritual beings which are an audience to our deeds. Those who are enemies of the Lord, specifically Satan and his followers, the fallen angels, many times have a front row seat to our sin. They may have even had a hand in tempting or stirring up our lusts in order that we did sin in a grievous way, but we are culpable. We mustn't think they are omnipresent as God is, but there are more eyes watching us then we might like to admit. It is always intriguing to read the account Satan has with God at the beginning in Job chap. 1. The whole dialogue between v.6 -12 is very informative, but we see that Satan is going to and fro upon the earth and walking up and down on it. Peter calls him our adversary, walking about seeking as a lion whom he might devour. We could look at other passages, but we must always realize that our sin gives these enemies of God and man much to blaspheme about.

Lastly, and perhaps most importantly, God confronts us in order that we may be made aware of our need for repentance. Sometimes we need to be strongly reminded of this for we so easily forget. And this is why we say that confrontation with God is a blessing or grace in that it demonstrates the love of God. God is patient towards all, not wishing that any should perish, desiring that all should come to repentance (see 2Peter 3:8-10) God's kindness is meant to lead you to repentance (Romans 2:3-4), and many other verses throughout the Bible demonstrate the lovingkindness of God, and how He is longsuffering; but there is a day of judgement.

It is a blessing for believers who have repented and believed, in that confrontation or chastisement is a sign that we are members of the household of God; we have been adopted into His family, and are considered sons. Hebrews 12 goes into this further, and it is truly a blessing when we are chastised by the Lord, even though as we all might attest to, it is not necessarily pleasant to go through. And while it would be nice to spend some time here contemplating the great love with which God loves us by doing this I want to spend a few moments speaking to those who have spurned this love.

For now we will not speak of those who have never heard of salvation through faith in Christ, it is another subject for another time. But those reading or listening to this have been blessed with hearing the gospel, or the good news that Christ came to save sinners, yet some of you still refuse to repent and believe. I want to take you back to Romans 2 for a moment. In fact it would be beneficial to read chapter one and two, but we will look at just a couple of verses in chap. 2. Why do you despise the riches of His goodness, why do you despise the riches of forbearance, why do you despise the riches of His longsuffering? Have you not been told more than once that the goodness of God leads to repentance? But in accordance with your hardness and your impenitent heart you are treasuring up for yourself wrath in the day of wrath and revelation of the righteous judgement of God. But despite all that we are here once again, and God through us is proclaiming the need to repent and believe in the Lord Jesus Christ for salvation from the wrath that is coming upon all the ungodly for their sin. It is a blessing that He allows you to hear once again; today is the day of salvation and yet you waver. And why is it that you waver, knowing that soon, probably sooner than we wish, you must stand before God and give an account? Is it the sin you love, or that enmity against God you were born with, or are you like the evil one who says surely you will not die, knowing full well that you will?

Some of you are more crafty and scheming and will play lawyer ball and say that unless God gives you a heart to believe, you cannot believe, and true, scripture teaches this. But if this is so, and you desire salvation, why are you not crying before God day and night to change your heart in order that you might believe? It is because you do not want to believe. You know it is true, but you will not submit to that authority of God which He is entitled to.

But there is coming a day in which the confrontation of God will not be a blessing for you, but a curse, and He will say to you depart from Me you workers of iniquity into the lake of fire created for the devil and his demonic cohorts. It is a day when the words "Abandon all hope ye who enter here" will be sealed upon you, and in that moment it will all become very clear. But that day is not here yet, and so there is still time. Run to Christ for forgiveness and believe while it is still called today. May these words penetrate your heart, and may you come to understand the love and forgiveness of God which surpasses all understanding. Shalom.

ELECTION AND SIN

One of the primary purposes of these short articles or writings, whatever you want to call them, is to encourage the disciple of Christ as he or she walks through this pilgrimage that we call life. Many of the things we speak about are nothing new, or at least they shouldn't be for most of you, but often times it is necessary to remind ourselves of just who we are, and what it means to be "in Christ." Now I realize and you do too, that we cannot in these short writings give full explanations of everything, and as we forward these to others who may be unbelievers it brings up other questions that need to be answered. It should be each one of our desires that all those whom we come into acquaintance would hear and understand the gospel. That doesn't mean they will believe, but they will understand.

Now as I am writing this, I am listening to some music, and one of the songs which came on a moment ago is one that we can all relate to, and that is "Why me Lord?" And it continues to ask what have I ever done to deserve even one of the pleasures that I have known? Do you ever ask the question, why me Lord? It is the answer to this question that should humble us and cause us too continually seek to glorify God in our lives and in all of our being and that is the doctrine of election. Of course most new believers in Jesus have never heard of election, but unfortunately many long time followers of Jesus haven't heard of it either. And of those who have, how many have an erroneous view of it? But a correct view not only tends to a greater glorification of God, it at the same time causes us to see in a greater way the heinousness of sin. While in this life we will never be rid of sin, a reminder of how evil it is, and the lengths God went through in the work of our salvation, will be an increasingly strong motive for us to rid all aspects of it out of our life. Mortification, not simply in the mind, but an active pursuit to kill all sin which remains in us; a lifelong struggle.

In some ways the doctrine of election is easy to understand, but the human side of us, that depraved nature that clings to us wants to say it isn't fair. Election simply says that before the creation of the world, God chose some to be the recipients of His grace in Christ (the salvation of our souls), simply from the good pleasure of His will, and not for anything which He foresaw that we would do. This sounds harsh to our human understanding, because if God chose some, it means there are others he didn't chose for salvation, and they have no hope. We could come up with several reasons why we think this is unfair, but probably the main reason we think it is unfair, is because we have an insufficient view of what sin really is. The real question everyone should be asking themselves, is why God should save anyone?

The bible, as well as our conscience, makes it very clear that all of us have sinned. It isn't really necessary to spend a lot of time on this because it is so clear, but because God's justice and righteousness demand that the penalty of sin be enforced upon the guilty, who can escape judgement since we are all guilty from the moment of birth? Most of you who read these little articles are completely aware of this so it shouldn't be necessary to spend a lot of time on those verses which prove these things, but if necessary, just let us know. This judgement, this penalty of sin is death; physical, which except for two exceptions that I know of, all of us must go through, spiritually, for we were born spiritually dead, and the eternal death which is the everlasting punishment for sin. Think a moment what it means to be everlastingly punished for your sin. That is the state that every individual that has ever been born or will be born is destined to, and why? Because we have sinned against God and that is the just penalty for our disobedience.

But God; if you are not intimately familiar with the first two chapters of Ephesians you should do so, but God, being rich in mercy, because of the great love with which he loved us, even when we were dead in our trespasses, made us alive together with Christ-by grace you have been saved through faith, and this faith is the gift of God.

When we first become believers, we have that faith that Jesus died for our sin, and we are no longer under the impending wrath of God that is sooner or later going to becoming upon the world. But it is usually something that we think we have done ourselves. It is upon reaching that aha moment when we truly realize that the faith we have has been given to us by God, and we must ask why; why me Lord? And the short answer is to the praise of the glory of his grace. Not because we were good or did anything special, or because we (in our own mind) weren't as bad as the next guy, but simply for his own will and for the praise of the glory of his grace. That is a phrase worth meditating a long time on.

But if faith is a gift of God and it is not a gift He gives to all men, and it is not a gift based on merit, then it is a gift that He sovereignly gives to whosoever He wills, and he gives it to those whom He has chosen to give it to before the foundation of the world, and so we say, these are His chosen ones, the elect.

We aren't going to go into all the nuances of this, but the doctrine of election brings along with it a great assurance that if you have true faith in Christ, your salvation is sure. We only have to look in Romans 8 to see this ordo salutis, this order of salvation, and realize it is all a work of God from start to finish. And if all this is so, why are you still sinning? When I say that I realize that there is no perfection this side of the grave, but how many of us live in many ways with a loose view of sin? Sometimes it seems like an oscillating wave, sometimes we are very conscious of sin and do our best to mortify it, but then we look again and we are once again taking it lightly. And this should humble us. Why did God choose me or choose you instead of choosing somebody else when we were both sinners by birth? That old saying "there but for the grace of God go I", is a very true statement. It should give us pause in how we view our fellow man. We didn't do anything to deserve this, so let us humble ourselves under this grace.

Election should be a great deterrent to sin, because it was sin that got us into this mess in the first place, and why now, after all that God has done in behalf of our salvation are we returning to it. God chose us to be different; we are sanctified, set apart, so why remain thinking and acting like those who haven't been? It is when we realize that we had nothing to do with our salvation, and that it was a sovereign act of God, and that He continues to work in us, that we will begin to understand the love that goes beyond understanding that He has for us.

I wish there were pages and pages I could write on this, because what we have discussed only scratches the surface and is very incomplete. But the intention is to get ourselves to remember what God has done for us, and to have some serious introspection into how we are living our lives, and deal with it accordingly. These short writings are always incomplete, but may they cause you to think and glorify God.

Until next time, Shalom.

WHICH IS GREATER?

It is always interesting to see how grandparents sometimes teach their grandchildren, and it reminds me of a story I once heard. It so happened that on one occasion a grandson went to visit his grandpa after Sunday school, and naturally the grandfather asked the child what he had learned that day. "Well" said the young man, "we learned about the ten commandments."

"And what did you learn about them?" asked his grandfather.

"That some of them are about our duty to God and that some of them are about our duty to people" replied the grandson.

"Ah, yes" said the grandfather. "They teach us that we are to love the Lord our God with all our heart, soul and mind, and to love our neighbor as ourselves."

"But which is better grandpa" asked the child, "To love God with all our heart or to love our neighbor?"

The grandfather smiled and then asked in return, "Which is more important to the bird, the left wing or the right wing?"

Sometimes the greatest learning comes in words of simplicity. Babies as well as young believers need to be fed milk. But solid food, meat is reserved for those more mature. Many of us could come up with several verses dealing with this subject of loving our neighbor and loving God, and if 1 John 4:20 is not familiar to you, go and read it. Reading verses 7-21 would be even better.

This has been a busy week for many of us, and it would have been nice to do more posts, but I didn't know where to start. About ten different areas come to mind, and indecision led to nothing getting done. On a regular basis I listen to those who like to hear themselves talk, and to show their profundity in areas in which they have no learning. Can you hear the sarcasm dripping? And instead of using words of simplicity which all can understand, they confuse rather than edify the listener, using words which most of us never use. Maybe that is why they are on the internet and not the classroom. Perhaps it was after listening to this individual that simplicity was on my mind. Many of the biblical doctrines can be taught in a very simple way. That doesn't mean they don't need to be fully explained, it just means we must do so in a way which the hearer understands.

Parents and grandparents, but especially parents are given the task of diligently teaching their children the words of God. This is to be done at home, when opportunities arise outside the home, when they are put to bed and when they rise up. This goes for us as well, not just for the kids. But it can be done simply with everyday occurrences. We watch the birds working and flying around and singing and we know that God is taking care of them. And it should refresh our hearts knowing God is sovereignly taking care of us as well. It is those simple kinds of things which make a deep impression upon the minds of children, and I hope us as well.

Anyway, maybe next week will be more productive on this end, and hopefully all of you are doing well. Until next time, Shalom.

MEDITATING ON THE MEDIATION

How often do you meditate on the mediation of Christ? Realizing that many of you who read these posts are not Christian it may seem as if this doesn't concern you, but in fact it does. In this post we are going to explore some basic facts that most of us know who are Christians, but it never hurts to go back and refresh our memory from time to time. 1Timothy 2:5 tells us that "there is one God and one Mediator between God and man, the Man Christ Jesus, who gave himself a ransom for all" We went a little into v. 6, but we get the idea; there is only one Mediator.

To keep this post short, we aren't going to deviate into all the nuances of mediation, or to answer those critics that say intercessory prayers on our part is comparable to the mediation of Christ. It simply isn't true. However we are going to briefly look into why Jesus' mediation is efficient and why He is the only mediator between God and man. Why is He qualified and no one else is. We are going to try and leave out as much theological jargon as we can, and leave this elementary in explanation if possible, while at the same time making it clear. But to begin, why is a mediator necessary and what is Jesus mediating?

Now if you don't know what a mediator is, it is simply a party or individual in this case, who is tasked with bringing two opposing sides into an agreement, or to settle differences. He is a representative qualified (and we are looking primarily at our case here of God vs. man) to speak on the behalf of man, and at the same time qualified by God to speak on His behalf. And this is where it should be exciting to those of you who have never thought about it this way before, and for those who have, it should never lose its wonder.

No ordinary man could come before God as a mediator. Say you are in a union and in negotiations with management for something like better working conditions. Not always, but typically the union representative is chosen from among the workers to speak on their behalf. So in the situation we are looking at, who chose Jesus to be our representative, and how is he qualified to do so? Well, let's back up a moment and see first what is being mediated. To keep it simple so we don't have to write a book, peace and reconciliation are being mediated. It is not quite this simple, but man is suing for peace. Now what is interesting about all this is that man is really not suing for peace; he is at enmity with God, and is quite satisfied to stay in that state. All men for the most part are ignorant of this fact and those who are not ignorant usually are unconcerned with the consequences. They don't understand the heinous and treasonous act that sin really is, and again, most could care less. And this is where the great lovingkindness of God (hesed) is demonstrated. Romans 5:8 says that "But God demonstrates His own love for us in that while we were still sinners, Christ died for us." Or that passage in 2 Corinthians 5 which culminates by saying that God was in Christ reconciling the world to Himself. So our case is really not man reaching out to God, but God reaching out to man saying, "Come let us reason together."

But who will be the representative for mankind? It cannot be an ordinary man, for all men are in the same state. It is written that all have sinned, so we are all born into the same state of enmity, and have the same need for someone to intercede on our behalf. Before we go on there might be some who say so what? Why do I need to be reconciled to God or to be at peace with Him? I don't bother him, and he doesn't bother me; just let me live my life how I want. Most of us have heard or even said something like this in the past, and while we mention it in many posts, it is necessary to say it as often as needed. The penalty for sin is death; physical, spiritual, and eternal, and eternal death is not annihilation as some would wish, but an eternity enduring the wrath of God against you for your sin. Now you may scoff at this to your own peril, but you have no excuse for not knowing. And even if these posts do not make it as clear as you would like, you are always free to ask for greater clarity either here or somewhere else, but it is impossible to plead ignorance.

Back to our question of who is qualified to represent mankind? Since it cannot be a sinner who needs reconciliation for himself, it therefore needs to be someone who was not only born sinless, but lived a sinless life in thought and deed, neither committing or omitting any of the requirements that would be necessary in living that sinless life. Now say that was possible for an ordinary human being to do. Is that not what is required of all of us, to love the Lord our God with all our heart, soul, mind and strength and to love our neighbor as ourselves? So anyone fulfilling all those requirements is simply doing that duty which we are all bound to do, but can't. It is possible that individual could speak for themselves, but what would give them the right to speak on the behalf of others? It could only happen if God chose or appointed or to use the biblical term, anointed that individual to be the spokesman for mankind. And such is the case when we speak of Jesus. He is the anointed one, the messiah, the Christ. He was truly man, but when we look at his miraculous birth, we see that He was also truly God. Those of you who are Christian know this to be true, and if there are some reading this who aren't, and want to know more, just ask. These posts are much too short in which to give a full explanation of every detail.

In simplistic and incomplete terms, as God, whatever Jesus did would have infinite worth, and as man, he could fulfill all the requirements needed on our behalf in which to be reconciled to God. The doctrine of imputation is simply that Christ's righteous life is accounted to believers, and it is as if we had lived a perfect life. But there was still a need for the payment of the penalty we had incurred for sin, and so God placed our sin, or imputed our sin to Christ, and He bore the punishment for it. In that way God's justice would be satisfied for the penalty which sin incurs. As man, Jesus endured the wrath of God, and as God it had infinite worth.

Now when Jesus died upon the cross it was as our substitute, and as to all the particular details involved between He and God the Father, we are not privy to all that transpired. But we do know from scripture that God's wrath against sin was satisfied, and Jesus' perfect life was reckoned to out account. BUT, there is a condition. Jesus came to save those who would believe. We all know John 3:16, For God so loved the world that He gave His only begotten Son, that whosoever would believe in him would not perish, but have eternal life.

Jesus died on the cross as a substitute, and in three days rose again from the dead. Do you believe? We have only touched on this today, and volumes could and have been written on the subjects mentioned, but it really does boil down to the simple fact of faith. Believe in the Lord Jesus Christ and you will be saved.

Many years ago I taught a small group of men on this topic, and it was a blessing to all of us. To meditate on the mediation of Christ, and all that is involved in His so doing, is something we should all do on a regular basis. Think on these things, and if we can help in anyway, please feel free to ask.

Until next time, Shalom.

THE DEITY AND WORK OF THE HOLY SPIRIT

When it comes to the deity and work of the Holy Spirit, a lot of Christians are somewhat confused as to whom He is, and what He does. There seems to be a vagueness about the whole idea. Perhaps this is because we can somehow visualize God the Father, and the Son, Christ Jesus, is also easy to picture. But how do we create in our minds a Spirit? It can become even more confusing when we read what Jesus said to the women at the well in John 4:24. "God is Spirit and those who worship Him must worship in spirit and truth." We don't tend to think of a person as someone we can't see. Yet the Holy Spirit is a Person, one of the three persons in the Trinity of the One God, not a second class citizen. It is imperative that we recognize that the Holy Spirit IS God, and not just a force or an "it."

Perhaps the most well-known passage concerning the deity of the Holy Spirit is found in Acts 5:3-4. A man named Ananias and his wife Sapphira had sold some land. But when Ananias brought the proceeds to the Apostle Peter, it was not the amount which he and his wife had promised to give to God. Listen to what Peter tells Ananias and consider, have you ever done anything similar?

"Ananias, why has Satan filled your heart to lie to the Holy Spirit and keep back part of the price of the land for yourself? While it remained, was it not your own? And after it was sold, was it not in your own control? Why have you conceived this thing in your heart? You have not lied to men but to God."

Peter equates here lying to the Holy Spirit the same as lying to God. So the Holy Spirit is God, or it wouldn't make sense. Let's look for a moment though at the consequences of lying to the Holy Spirit. If we read further in that passage in Acts, it says that when Ananias heard these words he fell down and died. Then a few hours later his wife came in and upon being questioned on how much the land was sold for, assented to what her husband had brought in. Again, listen to Peter's reply. "How is it that you have agreed together to test the Spirit of the Lord?" Then immediately she died also.

We will give a couple of more verses having to do with the Holy Spirit being God in a moment, but we can't leave this passage without asking ourselves a few questions. For starters, how did Satan fill their hearts to lie to the Holy Spirit? We can come up with all kinds of scenarios, but I tend to imagine that they sold that parcel of land for more than they originally thought they could get. And since it says that the proceeds were in their control after the land was sold, this lying must have come afterwards. Apparently, they said something to the effect that they had sold their land, and would give it all to the Lord. But when we look at Peter's reply again, we realize they weren't just lying to men, but to God. What caused them to change their mind from the time they promised the proceeds and the time that they actually brought It.?

It says that Satan filled their hearts to lie, but how did he do that? It just goes to show us that as it says in Ephesians, we are to put on the whole armor of God. I encourage you to read Ephesians 6:10-18, for we are in a hand to hand combat with spiritual hosts of darkness, and it is only the power of God in us that can resist. And without that armor, we can be easily be defeated in our daily walk with Christ. If Satan can so easily cause them to lie to God, how often has he caused us to do similar? I am sure all of us could, if we were honest, come up with instances where we have lied to God.

But moving on, we see the consequences of lying to the Holy Spirit, and that was death. It doesn't say days or weeks or years, but immediately. So why don't we see that happening today? For one thing it was given as an example. When we lie to God, it is serious business. And whether we lie to the Father, or to Jesus, or to the Holy Spirit, it is still lying to God. As believers in Christ, why would we lie to God? We need to move on, but ponder that question in your heart, for if we would be totally honest, must of us have lied to the Holy Spirit in one way or another. Back to our question of why we don't see that happening today, and it could be that too many people would be dropping dead. This is serious business we are talking about and most of us don't tend to take these sorts of things as seriously as we should. But this incident is given in order that we might see the seriousness of lying to God. Also, it could be that a lot of people are having consequences directly related to lying to the Holy Spirit that we just don't see. It has been said many times before that sometimes the consequence of sin is sin. May we look at this passage and see that not only that the Holy Spirit is God, but examine our own lives and see if we are in any way lying to God.

We could continue and look at several of the verses we find in John chapters 14-17, which intimate that the Holy Spirit is God. Also in these verses we see a personality when it speaks of the Spirit of Truth from the Father, who is a Helper. Passages which say "He will bear witness of me" or as in John 16:13 where it says "When the Spirit of truth comes, He will guide you into all truth, for He will not speak on His own authority, but whatever He hears He will speak, and He will declare to you the things that are to come." Verses 14-15 have similar ideas, that we are viewing here not a force but a person. These are just a few instances but throughout scripture we have references to the Spirit of God, or sometimes when God is speaking He says He will send His Spirit among them, and give them new hearts. Search the scriptures and you will begin to be amazed at the number of places the Spirit of God or the Holy Spirit is referred to.

This barely scratches the surface of what could be said, and there are some really good books out there for further study on this topic. The Work of the Holy Spirit by Abraham Kuyper or The Holy Spirit by Sinclair Ferguson are two worth reading, but there are many others out there as well. And here we should perhaps give ourselves a warning. When we study Theology, and those topics which fall into its prevue, it should not be so that we might become more knowledgeable about something, a topic, but that we might become more acquainted with our God. And we cannot start at a better place than where He has revealed Himself, and that is in the pages of the Bible. This is one of those places where we see the Holy Spirit at work.

Earlier we read that when the Spirit of Truth comes He would guide us into all truth. One of the ways He does that is in the words of scripture of which He is its author. Two verses, 2 Timothy 3:16 and 2 Peter 1:21 are especially relevant. In Timothy we read that "All scripture is breathed out by God..." and in Peter it says that "No prophecy was ever produced by the will of man, but men spoke from

God as they were carried along by the Holy Spirit." The bible, though penned by the hand of men, is authored by non-other than God the Holy Spirit.

It is not only through reading the Word of God that we are enlightened as to whom God is and what His will for our life is, but also by the hearing of the word through preaching. We have mentioned it before, but the passage in Romans 10 is especially relevant, because for one it says faith comes by hearing, and hearing by the word of God. Some versions read through the word of Christ, but if there is no one to proclaim the gospel, how can one be saved? "How beautiful are the feet of those who preach the good news!" It is just another example of how important missions are, and our own efforts at evangelism. I am so negligent in this area, as well as many of you are. But we need to constantly remind ourselves that we may be the only avenue through which lost people may ever hear the gospel.

Nevertheless, spiritual things must be spiritually discerned, and as it says in 1 Corinthians 2:14, "The natural person (those not regenerated or born again) does not accept the things of the Spirit of God, for they are folly to him, and he is not able to understand them because they are spiritually discerned." So how does someone believe that good news of the gospel if it is foolishness to him?

There are many works of the Holy Spirit that we could look at, all of them important, but the one that concerns us most, is in our regeneration. As Jesus told Nicodemus in John chapter 3, "Unless a man is born again, he cannot see the Kingdom of God." We must be born of the Spirit, and that is only something God can do. This is one of the works of the Holy Spirit. Regeneration must come before anyone can hear or understand the gospel of Jesus Christ. Faith is a gift of God that comes through hearing, but not until we have been born again with new ears to hear. It is the Holy Spirit working in us, creating in us a new heart that we might be able to believe the gospel, and through faith in the gospel be saved.

There is a great passage in Ezekiel 36 that speaks on this, and I recommend reading and meditating on the WHOLE chapter, but in verses 26-27 we see that work which only God can do for those dead in their trespasses and sin.

"And I will give you a new heart, and a new spirit I will put within you. And I will remove the heart of stone from your flesh and give you a heart of flesh. And I will put my Spirit within you, and cause you to walk in my statutes and be careful to obey my rules." (ESV)

It is written in one of the Apostle Paul's letters that if we have been born again, we are a new creation. This is not something we can or could do, but is solely an act of God. Why would God recreate us in order that we could believe the gospel? More than once we have contemplated and answered this, and we could go on into more detail even now, but until we meet next, ask God, Why me Lord?

Shalom

PRACTICAL ATHEISM

There are a lot of people who have never heard the name Jesus, but there are many more that have heard, and reject Him as a Savior, or think that He never even existed. The majority believe He probably existed, but do not think He was who He claimed to be, or who and what the bible declares Him to be. The idea of a Trinity is completely ridiculous in their minds, and that Jesus is God is even more so. C.S. Lewis said that when we look at the claims of Jesus, we must see that He is either a liar, a lunatic or LORD.

While writing this, I was reminded of an occasion when I happened to be in a location where I shouldn't have been. There were probably 50-100 people milling about, but there was a lady (?), perhaps better to call her female, who was drunk and loud and talking to be talking, and to nobody in particular. I'm not sure exactly what happened, but she said it had to be evil. Remember, she was drunk, and I mean very drunk, and whether it was evil or not, she said it was the work of Satan, the devil. She then went on to say she believed that the devil was real and caused all of these evil things, but then went right into blaspheming Jesus. Again, she wasn't talking to anyone in particular, but she started saying how she believed in the devil and God, but not Jesus, and that Jesus wasn't a real person, and the bible was just a bunch of lies to keep people enslaved. Those weren't her exact words, but you get the gist. She didn't mention much about God, if at all, but I am sure she said something. The point being, that there are millions upon billions of people in the world who don't know or don't believe in Jesus, but do believe in a God.

(Just as an aside, as a Christian, we should say something at such occasions, even if we know we are alone or definitely in the minority. I must admit I did not, and it bothers me even now when I am writing this. Are we ashamed? I have prayed for this lady and ask that you would as well. Perhaps one day she shall stand beside us praising the grace of God.)

Getting back to these billions that believe in a God. This God that they do believe in may not be the God we see revealed in Holy Scripture, but they do believe in some sort of god.

With that being said, we also realize that there are a multitude of people who claim to be atheists. But really, what kind of atheists are they? In all instances, every human being has a sense of what is right and wrong, good and evil. True, we don't always see eye to eye on everything, but we all have some sort of moral code. Now think with me for a minute, who determines what is right and what is wrong, what is good and what is evil? Without an ultimate authority (God) to determine this, the terms are non-existent. But that is not our concern today. Our purpose for today is with the mass of humanity, whether churched or unchurched, who are practical atheists; they live their lives as if God didn't exist.

Some of you may be familiar with Stephen Charnock, a preacher who wrote and lived in the 1600's. Among his writings was a large piece on practical atheism. You may be able to find it online, and if you can, we recommend you read it. It will do you more good then you could imagine. But as a disciple of Christ you may ask, what has this got to do with me? At all times we need to examine our lives, especially before we come to the ordinance of the Lord's Supper, and one of the things we need to ask, am I in the faith? Of course we say yes, but does the living out of our life say different? Actions speak louder than words.

Now it is admitted that not everyone has a dramatic conversion experience. There are a lot of factors involved, age being perhaps the greatest. The older we get, the more we may become entrenched in certain sins, while those in their youth may not have learned them yet. So when we see someone who has been living in a sinful lifestyle come to Christ, usually there is a dramatic change. But does this change continue, and as for those saved when they were young, do they slowly lose interest in the things of Christ? When we look at our lives and don't see a significant difference between how we live and unbelievers live, we need to ask why? Sanctification, or the process by which we are made more and more like Christ, is not a straight line upwards. There are many peaks and valleys, but in those valley times we are in a sense living as if God doesn't exist. I probably could have explained that a little better, but when you and I sin, there is a sense in which we are telling God that His rules are not important.

There is that spirit of atheism in every sin we commit. If we really believed that God has set rules or guidelines by which we are to live, and Has revealed Himself to mankind in the bible, there is no way you would break those rules, knowing the consequences of doing so. Yet we do it every day, and not only that, but multitudes of times every day. So we know God exists, but we live as if He didn't.

There are a couple of other things we will briefly consider today, one of which is that when we sin, or set the rules for our own life, we are in charge, not God. That isn't really the case, but we think it is, and are like the kid that says "You aren't the boss of me." So is God wrong and we are right in how we chose to live life? If He really exists, then doing or thinking anything other than what He has declared is in essence saying it doesn't matter. And, if it doesn't matter, than practically you are saying God doesn't exist. Your mouth says He does, but your life says differently.

Sometimes I read over these articles before I post them and think I should delete it all and try again; such is todays. But I will leave it as it is, and just ask one final question. Are you living your life as if God doesn't exist? Think on this and act accordingly, and until next time, Shalom.

REGENERATION: A WORK OF THE HOLY SPIRIT

It has been a couple of weeks now since we have been in our study of theology, and we now return to our topic of soteriology. In simple terms, this is the study of salvation and doctrines related to that. We briefly looked at the fact that it is by the grace of God that anyone is saved, and this grace is being given a new heart and will, in order that we might believe the message of the gospel, and chose Christ as our Savior. Without being given a new heart and a new will, no man can choose Christ, nor will want to choose Christ. We call this act, regeneration, or being born again, and as it says in Ezekiel 36:26, God will give us a new heart and a new spirit he will put within us. He will remove the heart of stone from our flesh, and give us a heart of flesh. There may be some who will object and say that this passage is God speaking to the house of Israel, the physical nation of Israel. But a careful reading of chapter 36 and 37, will make it clear that God is speaking to the Church, those who constitute the House of Israel, which is all those who are of the household of faith, from the beginning of time, to the final return of Christ. This matter is more defined in the New Testament, and when we come to ecclesiology, we will mention it again, as some find difficulty with the term the house of Israel as it refers to the church in the New Testament era.

But getting back to our topic of regeneration, it is only after we have been given a new heart and a new will, that the calling of the gospel message will be effective, and we will have faith in its truth. It is only then that true repentance and the resulting fruits will begin. As we mentioned last time, there are some groups out there who believe that because of the atoning work of Christ, God has given all men sufficient grace in order to believe the gospel and be born again, but this reverses the order and makes it a work of man, not a sovereign work of God. This also skews up the doctrine of election, for if a man may or may not choose repentance and faith, then it is not up to God, but the man choosing or not choosing. This is contrary to everything the Bible teaches about election and the sovereignty of God, and the deadness or depravity of the human condition. We have addressed this somewhat in previous articles, but if someone desires further clarification, please feel free to ask. This is a serious and can be a difficult topic at times, especially in our format, so it is not easy to address every nuance. But the one thing we will address today, as it seems to garner the most attention, and that is, if God's call or command for all men to repent and believe the gospel is genuine. Let us see if we can draw up the question in its totality.

God knows and reveals through his word, that no man will believe the gospel call, unless he gives them a new heart (regeneration) to believe. Therefore, is God being sincere when he calls a man to repent and believe in Christ for the forgiveness of sin and eternal life, knowing that he will not give him a heart to believe? This is not a new question, but has been asked down through the ages, and will continue to be asked. It is a legitimate question, and while we can give an answer, it is not always one which soothes the listener's heart. In some cases it even hardens the heart, which perhaps for some it is the design. Even Christians sometimes misunderstand or maybe confuse certain issues involved here, and as a result, evangelism suffers. We will get into all of this either today or next time, but for now, is God being sincere?

We say yes, for God promises salvation to all who hear the gospel call and respond with faith and repentance. That there are those who are still unbelieving and unrepentant after hearing the gospel call, is not God's fault, but the hard heart of the hearer. His will does not want to choose Christ. This is why we say salvation is of the grace of God, for no man without a change of heart, willingly comes to Christ. Yet God in his mercy and grace, for the pleasure of his own good will, chooses some that he gives a new heart in order to believe. They in no way deserve this or have done anything of their own doing that merits salvation, so that it might be a sole work of God. Yet, it is the duty, and a reasonable duty for all men to repent and believe, for all have sinned and are under the wrath and condemnation of God. Those who remain in this state, do so because they want to, for otherwise, they would choose Christ. We are still under the obligation to obey the command of God, whether we like it or not, or even if by our sin we have destroyed the moral ability to do so. We could go in circles here, but let's

112

move on to the response we are most likely to hear when people realize the implication of what we have just stated. That is not fair they will say.

Perhaps one of the most sobering statements in scripture can be found in Romans 9:19-24, especially v.20. "But indeed, O man, who are you to reply against God?" Think about it, can the thing that has been created really have a right to say to the creator, why did you create me like this? And we so easily forget that originally we were created sinless, yet by our own free will, we transgressed the law of God. We will close with those thoughts for today, and continue next time with the next couple of questions that always arise, and that is the duty of prayer and evangelism. You have probably already figured out the question, but we will wait and ask it in our following post. May you have a blessed weekend. Shalom.

REGENERATION CONTINUED

Welcome back to our study in theology. It has been a rough two or three weeks trying to get back on a routine of writing. Several events have occurred in life recently that has caused a necessary change of my daily habit, and unfortunately this is one of those areas that have suffered the consequences. Though there may only be a handful that actually read and benefit from this study, it would be a dereliction of duty just to quit mid-stream. We had ended our last post with the question that everyone seems to ask when it comes to regeneration, election and predestination. That is, what is the point in our doing anything? If God has chosen who will be saved, which we call election, what point is it in proclaiming the gospel, and the question which goes right along with it, and that is why pray? This seems on the surface a legitimate question, but it really isn't as we shall soon see.

As stated last time, before an individual will choose to believe the gospel, God must change their heart. I do not think it is necessary to go over again why this is so, but if anyone has forgotten or needs clarification, please feel free to ask. However, at the same time we must admit, that for a large proportion of the Christian community, they have been taught different. In many circles it is taught or assumed, that it is after one believes that God changes the heart, not before. But where is the sovereignty of God in that? All of a sudden salvation becomes a work of man which God is obligated to reward, and grace is no longer grace but a reward for faith. Paul deals with this in numerous places, Galatians and Ephesians 2:8-9 come to mind right off, for it is by grace we have been saved, not of works, but it is the gift of God. It is not necessary to go any further at this time, but this is where our question comes in, why evangelize, if God is going to do it all anyway?

In God's decree, that decree where he has determined what will come to pass, by the pleasure of his own good will, he has decided that say John Smith will be the recipient of eternal life. All of this has happened before the foundation of the earth, but obviously, John doesn't know that does he? But how is this to happen? God has also decreed the means by which this is to happen, and that is by John hearing, or in some cases reading the gospel of how Jesus came to save sinners, and by faith, John believes it. That God has chosen this way to reach out to men, should be a good enough reason for us to evangelize, and not only that, but by using men as this secondary way if you will, God has given us the privilege of being involved with this great work. As has been stated in scripture, one plants and another waters, but it is God who gives the increase. Romans 10 is a great declaration of this also, which we cannot overlook. We may mention this again next time when we look at justification, but as it says, everyone who calls upon the name of the Lord will be saved. But, how will they call on him in whom they have not believed? And how are they to believe in him of whom they have never heard? And how are they to hear without someone preaching?

This is God's way of reaching the lost sinner, the means he has chosen to call his own to himself, and because he uses the means of preaching to reach out or call to faith his elect, we go out and preach. And if this is the means he has chosen, that should be good enough reason in itself. To go much further and question why do something which God has commanded, is obviously putting yourself in a position you don't want to be in. The same goes with prayer. It is the means which God has chosen for us to communicate with him. It is in the book of James that it says the fervent prayer of a righteous man availeth much, and we have so many examples in scripture, that it shouldn't even be a question at all. It is too easy to play the game of what if here, and when we do, it usually ends up badly. Think of the many times Moses interceded or prayed on behalf of the Israelites. To say what if he had not have done so is somewhat ridiculous, for we don't know what would have happened, but we do know what happened because of his intercession. We have examples like this in order to encourage us to pray. It is one of the secondary means God uses, and is such a large part, or should be, of our Christian walk that to not do so should seem foreign to our way of thinking. We could speak much more on this subject, and it is interesting, but it can lead to speculation if we are not careful, and we have really said all that is necessary.

In truth, these questions we are looking at are really only ever raised by either those who are unbelievers looking for some type of reason to continue in their unbelief, or perhaps justify it, and those who believe that all men have the capacity or capability to believe if the right persuasion is used. That God is sovereign in who will or who will not believe is foreign to their way of thinking. True it can be a hard doctrine, but the means God has chosen is through the proclamation of the gospel, so we go out and proclaim it. We have no idea who God has chosen to salvation or when, so we proclaim it to all. We have already dealt with the issue of those who hear the gospel, but God has chosen not to regenerate, and how it is a genuine call to repentance, so we will not go over it again, unless asked to do so. We will probably touch on it again when we look at justification, which hopefully we will begin looking at next time.

As I always say in these posts from time to time, these are not meant to fully exhaust all the details of each of these subjects, and if there are any questions please feel free to ask, and hopefully we can answer them. The proper study of theology helps make it clear the great glory of God in all his workings, especially in our salvation, and while sometimes we may get bogged down in certain concepts and definitions, it is the glory of God we are really looking at.

In closing, think of the wondrous things that can be gleaned from that very first statement which God has revealed to us in his holy word.

"In the beginning, God created the heavens and the earth." Until next time, Shalom.

JUSTIFICATION

We have now come to the topic of justification in our studies, and as it has been in some of our other areas we have looked at, it seems an inadequate forum for discussing such an important aspect of our salvation. In some ways it seems as if it should be a simple topic, especially if we look at its simple definition, but it tends to raise other related issues, that many find not so clear. In most instances, the term justification is used in the sense that an individual is in conformity to the law. For our purposes, this is especially meant in the moral sense, in that the demands of the law of God have been met. Yet by defining it in this way, it may be misleading in that it is somehow a morality on our part, so it is better to say that justification should be used in a forensic sense. If we don't there is a chance of confusing it with sanctification.

God considers us just, because our relationship as it stands judicially before the law which he has placed before us, has been perfectly fulfilled, and we are considered righteous. Our being regenerated gives us the ability and desire to have faith in Christ, being obedient to the gospel call, and it is in Christ that we receive our justification. It is here that I would like to insert a couple of quotes from the Westminster confession of faith. The first if from Chap.XI of justification, and the second will be from the larger catechism Q. 70 What is justification?

"1. Those whom God effectually calleth, He also freely justifieth: not by infusing righteousness into them, but by pardoning their sins, and by accounting and accepting their persons as righteous; not for anything wrought in them, or done by them, but for Christ's sake alone; nor by imputing faith itself, the act of believing, or any other evangelical obedience to them, as their righteousness; but by imputing the obedience and satisfaction of Christ unto them, they receiving and resting on Him and His righteousness by faith; which faith they have not of themselves, it is the gift of God."

"Q. 70. What is justification? A. Justification is an act of God's free grace unto sinners, in which he pardoneth all their sins, accepteth and accounteth their persons righteous in his sight; not for anything wrought in them, or done by them, but only for the perfect obedience and full satisfaction of Christ, by God imputed to them, and received by faith alone."

Just a few of the biblical texts which deal with this, and we will only mention a handful of them, are Rom. 8:30, Rom. 4:5-8, Gal. 2:16, Acts 13:38-30,

Rom. 3:22, 24-25. There are others, but what is clear, or at least should be, is that this is an act of grace on God's part toward those whom he has predestined for eternal life and effectually called. Another aspect which we must not miss, is that this righteousness is not our own, but the righteousness of Christ imputed to us, and that the faith we have is itself a gift from God. If we will just keep these in mind, we will not fall into some of those errors which always seem to follow the doctrine of justification around.

What causes these errors is by taking an incorrect view of those characteristics that accompany or are described of the righteous. Sometimes these errors come about by confusing justification and sanctification. Justification takes place one time and all at once, whereas our sanctification takes place over our entire lifetime, and is not completed in this life. Because justification removes the guilt of sin, and we are declared righteous, there are some who have the idea that we are somehow sinless now, which goes against all scriptural teaching. We need to remember that our justification takes place outside of us, but in and of itself does not change the inner life. This is within the realm of sanctification. Our regeneration, being made a new creature and having faith in Christ, and the attendant justification, are a work and declaration of God, but we dare not forget that it is the merits of Christ which have been given or imputed to us, not some work of our own.

Because our sin, whether past present or future are pardoned and there is no guilt or penalty (except for temporal consequences which are not removed), we cannot escape the fact that we continue to sin. We only have to look at the Lord's Prayer in Matt. 6 and the passages in 1 John, to see that we continue to ask for pardon and forgiveness of sin. Even Paul deals with this somewhat in Romans 7. Again we must stress that we are not righteous in and of ourselves, but we have been clothed with the righteousness of Christ, and though judiciously we are right before God, it does not stand to reason that our lives will perfectly reflect this; again this belongs to sanctification. We will speak more on this when we come to sanctification, but those who are justified, are also being sanctified. Though they are different, they must go hand in hand; sanctification must follow justification or justification has not taken place. This also helps dispel the idea that this doctrine leads to licentiousness.

Simply put, it is the righteousness and obedience of Christ imputed to us that is the meritorious cause and foundation of our justification with God. (As stated by Turretin, though in a question form.) While there are many other aspects to justification we could look at, these are the main points, and as I always state, if there are further questions, please feel free to ask and we will try to answer them. Because adoption also is connected with our justification, we will take a brief view of that, and then move on to sanctification. Until then, may God bless you, and may your life in turn, glorify God. Shalom

I WILL BE SATISFIED....

Satisfaction is one of the hardest attitudes to achieve, right up there along with contentedness. Now being content and satisfied are basically synonymous, but there is a slight difference. However it is so slight that for our purposes they could be interchangeable, but since the verse we are going to look at says satisfied, that is what we are going to go with. The verse we are going to look at is found in Psalm 17:15 and reads "As for me, I will see Your face in righteousness; I will be satisfied when I awake in Your likeness."

Recently I had been asked to speak a few moments on some of the Psalms, this one being one of them, but for reasons which need not be gone into, I have had to decline. Some men would rather be filled with the sound of their own words and thoughts than to be taught, and I not having the skill to teach through that, refuse to be a cause of disunity. I need to be satisfied and humbled to the point where any pride I have in this matter is dissipated; maybe it is not meant for me to teach in such a venue, but reserve it for internet blogs. Time will tell, but since I had already prepared several of these psalms in advance, some of it may leak out into these posts. We need to humble ourselves in all aspects of life and be satisfied in Christ.

Now even though none of those individuals read this, or at least to my knowledge they don't, it would not do well to post something very similar to what they may have heard someone else say a day or two before. But this verse and the one or two preceding it were ones which were of particular interest, so we will spend a few moments on those, and not the whole psalm.

In this psalm, which is a prayer of David, he is petitioning the Lord to rescue him from the evil and wicked man. The man who would follow God, and desires to be a man after God's own heart, is going to suffer some kind of persecution, and as we see in David's life, he had more than his share of it. But his help he knew came from the Lord, and we see much of this crying out to God for vindication from the wicked, in many of the psalms.

We have a description here of some of these wicked men, that they have fat hearts, which could be indicative of pride, which spouts forth in their speech, and they are like wild lions, seeking whom they might devour. But the description we want to focus on is that found in v. 14. These are the wicked men that have their portion in this life. And what is this portion? It is the lust of the eyes, the lust of the flesh, and the pride of life. God has filled their bellies with His hidden treasure. God has given or allowed them to gain great wealth and treasure, and they are satisfied with children and apparently leave a great inheritance to those who follow after them. There are some who have said that instead of being satisfied with children, it should be that their children are also satisfied by the wealth, but they go hand in hand.

But the key thing to realize is that their portion is in this life. How often do we envy those who have wealth and are seemingly at ease? We see this talked about in several of the psalms and proverbs especially psalm 73, and it is so easy to forget that this is their portion, and it is only temporary; for just a few short years. And by contrast, how often do we see the godly in poverty and destitution, barely scraping by? As it says in Hebrews, some were destitute, wandering about the deserts and mountains and living in dens and caves. We don't see much of this type of poverty here in the U.S. but we could picture Lazarus and the rich man which we read of in Luke 16. By today's standards, this rich man would probably have been well known for his parties, who knows, he might even have had his own reality show, and all the trappings we see of those who flaunt their wealth. But he would give it all up today, for one drop of water on that tormented tongue. And what of his name and offspring? Whether his name was Dives or not, who knows for sure, but we have no recollection of those who came after him.

The worst thing that could ever happen to anyone is if God satisfied them with His hidden treasure, but left the door of salvation closed. What is a vapor of life compared to an eternity of torment? What should it profit a man if he should gain the whole world, but lose his soul? Be careful of striving after riches instead of seeking for the kingdom of God, because you just might find what you are looking for.

But someday the wicked will perish, but those who are godly, those who are clothed in the righteousness of Christ, they will see God. And that is our hope in our daily struggles whatever they may be. And how is it we are to be satisfied? We shall be satisfied on that day when we awake in the likeness of Christ. We may hunger and thirst after righteousness in this life, crying out with Paul, who shall save me from this body of death, mourning over the remaining sins of our heart, which at times seems so overwhelming, but someday we shall be filled. Our bodies will awake from the sleep of death and be made like unto Christ. Is that not what we look forward to?

So with all the hustle and bustle of the day that so easily distracts us, and the clamoring of the world after our attention, it is so easy to throw up our hands in defeat and like the Rolling Stones, say "I can't get no satisfaction." When that happens, take a deep breath, slow down a bit and remember this psalm.

"I will be satisfied when I awake in your likeness."

Until next time, Shalom.

ADOPTION AND SANCTIFICTION

It has been two or three weeks now since we have posted anything on our study of theology, and I apologize for letting other things get in the way of our study. It is not good to let much time elapse in between topics, but at the same time, we have an eternity to become more acquainted with our Lord and God, Jesus. Spend a moment and think about that. An eternity lies before us, and as the children of God, we will get to know Him more and more, and this brief time we spend on earth in a corrupt state of sin, though regenerated and made righteous by Christ, is not enough time to realize the glory of it all. We are the children of God by faith, having been adopted into a family composed of all nations, tongues and tribes. In Christ, we have become co-heirs of all things pertaining to life and godliness. We could spend a lot of time talking about adoption, but I am afraid the splendor of it all is greater than this author is capable of describing it. We were hopeless and wandering around in darkness and despair, without hope and not knowing it, but God reached down and took us by the hand and said, come and follow me and I will give you rest. God is our Father. Again, words escape me, so I will leave it to others to further explain adoption, but let us talk a moment of sanctification.

Sanctification is a many faceted jewel, and while we will not be looking at every side of it, there are some very important details involved which have lead men astray into strange and erroneous doctrines. One of the greatest errors has been the idea of an immediate and complete perfection in this life, as opposed to the working out of our salvation. This is a large subject in itself, and I recommend that one read B.B. Warfield's work on perfectionism to understand it further, but without getting bogged down in another subject, let us start by giving a definition of sanctification.

We are not going to look at all the different verb forms etc. of the old testament word for sanctify, which is qadash, or its noun qodesh, and while there is some difference of opinion, the best use is "to cut". There are some who would say it is related to a meaning of "to shine", which in some sense could be viewed as glorification, but to cut is the best. To cut out or to make separate is the best way of viewing sanctification, as God has cut out or separated His people from the rest of the population. Similar to this idea is holiness. A separating out of an ordinary thing for religious of sacred purposes. I would like to insert a quote here by a man named Girdlestone, of whom I am not familiar, but I am sure it is Charles Girdlestone but in any case this is what he had to say. "The terms sanctification and holiness are now used so frequently to represent moral and spiritual qualities, that they hardly convey to the reader the idea of position or relationship as existing between God and some person or thing consecrated to Him; yet this appears to be the real meaning of the word."

There are many ways we could take this from here, but without writing an excessive amount on all the issues, it might be best to say that morally we are be separated from all that is sinful and impure, which includes those desires for those things of this world, such as pride and the lust of the flesh, and all other sinful appetites we used to find pleasure in. In regeneration we have been made new creatures, with a heart of flesh, we have faith in Christ and we have been justified, or made right with God, and we now desire to live a life set apart to God, and to become more Christ-like.

But we must also attribute our sanctification to God and not ourselves. We are to use the means God has provided, or to cooperate with the means He brings our way in order to be more like Christ. We are to "put off the old man", being mortified of the deeds of the flesh, and to "put on the new man" which as it says in Ephesians has been created in Christ Jesus for good works. This sanctification also affects the whole person, body, soul and mind, or as others put it the intellect, affections and will. Because we have been regenerated, sanctification must take place. And, because this is a work of God which begins in the inner being of a person, it cannot help but bursting outward or manifesting itself in the life of a believer.

Again, our duty is to use the means at our disposal in this process of sanctification, but not forgetting it is a work of God nonetheless. Some of those means are our exercise of faith, meditating on our reading of the scriptures, prayer and corporate worship. The Holy Spirit uses these means, and we neglect them to our peril. Whenever these means begin to fade in our life, and by that I mean we are not spending time in prayer and bible study, or if we are not attending worship services and hearing the preaching of the word, it probably means we are allowing sin to dominate some area of our life. Or, it could mean that regeneration has not occurred, and we were attracted to Christianity for something other than faith in Christ.

Because this is an important subject, we will deal with it further next time. Principally, we will look at some of the errors this topic has spawned, and touch again on our responsibility to use the means God has placed at our disposal. This relates to fruitfulness in the Christian life, but more on that next time. Normally there is not a lot of scripture verses given unless someone request them, but next time, quite a few will be given as the topic demands it more than some others. Again, if there are any questions, feel free to ask, and hopefully we can answer them.

Until next time, this morning and every day until we meet again, may God's face shine upon you. Shalom.

SANCTIFICATION#2

We are going to finish up our study in sanctification today, by remembering that we (those who are Christians) have been cut out or separated out if you will, from all of humanity by God's electing grace. God has chosen or elected us to be His people by the good pleasure of his will alone, and not for anything we have done or might do, but simply for the praise to the glory of his grace. Not only has He chosen us before the foundation of the world, (Eph.1) but likewise has provided the means necessary to accomplish the redemption of our soul and body. We have already discussed faith and regeneration, which necessitates justification, but following justification, there is sanctification.

Now part of the danger with which men have gone into error is separating these two into distinct and different acts of faith, rather than speaking of them or "stressing their inseparable connection."- L. Berkhof. When we receive the Holy Spirit, it is not partially, but fully, and there is no need of a second grace to attend sanctification, or to make it effective. This is why we must say and stress that our sanctification is a work of God, which we cooperate with. However, we are to use those means at our disposal to increase in sanctification. Some verses which are helpful here would be 2 cor. 7:1, Col.3:5-14, and 1Peter1:22. We are to put off the old sinful man, and put on the new, but this also is a work of God for He strengthens us to do it. There can be no sanctification without justification, and to do works which seem to have sanctifying value without justification is simply another aspect to the self-righteousness deeds which men do in order to try and justify themselves before God and their fellow man. But they forget or ignore what is clearly taught, and that is by the deeds of the law, no man is justified. Sanctification is the fruit of justification, not its author. Yet, when we see no use of the means for greater sanctification in our life and in the lives of others, it is an indicator that justification may have never taken place, which unfortunately we see happen quite frequently. So what are some of the means which the Holy Spirit uses to increase our sanctification, means which we are to co-operate with?

First we have the Word of God. Not only is this the scriptures which we are encouraged to read and meditate upon, (Ps.1), but also the hearing of the Word of God proclaimed to us by those ministers and teachers given to us by God for the edifying of His people, the church. These tend to go hand in hand, for it is necessary that you try and sit under that teaching which is of God, not the imaginations of men. Without a strong scripture base yourself, it is easy to be led into error by men who might have their own agenda or are not qualified for one reason or another. We will delve into this more when we look at the doctrine of the church. It tends to be a pet peeve of mine, which is dealt with extensively in The Pedigree of Ordination. But getting back to our topic, the Word of God is primary in our sanctification. Next would be the sacraments, which we will also speak of further at a later time, but they are as it were visible truths, representing acts which have happened in the life of the believer. These would be the Lords supper and baptism, and all they signify. Thirdly, we have the providence of God. This may not always be as clear as the other two, but events in the believers life, or possible the life of others can often times be used in leading us to live a more sanctified life. It really isn't necessary to give an example, for there are many, but suppose we see someone steal and then get sent to prison. While in prison bad things happen to them as well as friends and family turning their backs on them. We read in the scriptures that we are not to steal, and we see the consequences first hand and decide that God is right, and we do not steal. Somewhat related to this idea of providence, is chastisement. This also takes on many forms, as each of us could probably attest to, but many times it is necessary in order for God to direct our attention back to Him. No one likes being disciplined, but when we know it is from the hand of God, and that the Holy Spirit is trying to make us more Christ like, we should take comfort. Hebrews 12:4-11 should be one of those passages that is seared in the Christians mind. If you don't already have it memorized, at least read it and remember the gist of it; the Lord disciplines those whom He loves.

There is a lot more we could look at in all these areas of sanctification, but hopefully what little has been said has whet your appetite to study it further. But before completely leaving this topic, we need to again give that warning against the idea of perfectionism. The passage we just looked at in Hebrews begins with (v.4) "In your struggle against sin." Some versions have striving instead of struggle, but it is the idea here of a conscious battle against sin. This would not be necessary if we were in fact fully sanctified in this life (perfectionism), and we were without sin. The whole idea of perfectionism cannot be fully explained in a few words, and again I recommend reading B.B. Warfield's work on perfectionism. It may not answer everything, but it does give one a handle on some of the problems in the American church that have resulted as an offshoot of this type of thinking.

As I always say at the end of each of these topics, if you have any questions or comments, please feel free to ask. We spend such little time in each area that sometimes the need for clarification is in order, as well as the fact some may have a differing view and in such cases we need to go to more scripture proofs if necessary. Next time we are going to start ecclesiology, the study of the church. Hope you can join us, and until then Shalom.

THOU EXCELLEST THEM ALL

If memory serves me right, Yogi Berra once said that if he had known he was going to live this long, he wouldn't have gotten old. It is one of my favorite quotes, because for many of us, time goes by so fast. Our minds are still in our twenties, but our bodies tell a different story. Yesterday was another anniversary, and it was a reminder how fast life can go by. Most of us have many acquaintances, but only a handful of friends. Unfortunately the great majority of people only have one or two true friends, and this is not just at the present, but in their entire life. A friend is someone who loves you and you love them, no matter what. That doesn't mean you will always like them or they will like you, but that is just temporary. But deep down there is a bond that cannot be broken, even if unspoken. There is complete trust. I had thought of relating a story here, but since it might distract from my thoughts, I will pass it by. Just, a friend will do whatever is necessary.

Now this is not necessarily going to be a long post, but hopefully one which whoever might read this, will ponder. Those of you who know me have probably at one time or another heard me speak on Proverbs 31. So you know who I think King Lemuel is, and his mother, and the occasion for her teaching. But in v. 10 we have his mother saying, "Who can find a virtuous woman? For her price is far above rubies." Just as an aside, a really nice ruby or an excellent emerald beats a diamond any day, even a sapphire can give a diamond a run for its money, but a ruby far surpasses them all. But a virtuous women; she is more precious than any ruby.

Verses 1-12, set up the whole occasion of this event, verses 13-27, describe her, and the remainder praises her. But I want to focus on v. 23, 28 and 29. Verse 23, "Her husband is known in the gates when he sitteth among the elders of the land." We are not going to spend much time on this, but it could very well be intimated that the only reason he is known, or that he is invited to sit with the elders, is that his wife is so virtuous. It is not so much his qualities that are renowned, but hers.

And we conclude with vs. 28-29. "Her children rise up and call her blessed; her husband also, and he praises her." And verse 29 should be recognized as the husband speaking to his wife. "Many daughters have done virtuously, but thou excellest them all."

So to my friend of 41 years, may the Lord bless you and keep you and may His peace be upon you always. Shalom.

DISOBEDIENCE OR OBEDIENCE?

As nearly everyone is aware, the school year has begun, and for many it is a new phase of life. It could be the parents sending their children off for the first time, or those students entering a new school. Moving into a new level such as junior high to high school can be quite traumatic for some, but one of the most significant jumps is that from high school to college. Seventeen and eighteen year olds being thrust into an environment quite different than the one they are used too. Most of them are away from home for the first time, but even more significant, is that they are now solely responsible as to how they will perform. To put it more simply, they have suddenly become accountable. There is no one there to tell them what to eat or how to spend the hours in the day; they are off the leash so to speak. They are free to do as they wish.

Over the last several weeks I have spoken with several freshman students, one of whom I personally know, and they are all excited, yet at the same time nervous. Why they thought my advice was any better than the next persons is not clear, but I did what I could. These were not the exact words used for each individual, but obedience is the clearest path for a successful life. Obedience to what was the primary response, and it is obedience to truth. Now these posts on The Christian Disciple are of course religious in nature, and we will get to that in a moment, but being obedient to what we know is required of us is always the path of least resistance. This is true whether or not you are a Christian.

But for those couple of students who were Christian, as well as countless others, this time of their life is going to be particularly difficult when it comes to that area of being obedient to the word of God. There is an unpublished manuscript I had tucked away, called the Obedience of Faith, and there is a chapter in it dealing with this very idea. It took a while to find the quote I wanted to tell these students and here it is. It is by J. Alec Motyer, "Disobedience often begins at a point where obedience would be easy but we do not think it important."

There are many of us if we were honest, could easily agree with this statement, having lived it out. The number one difficulty will be for them to find a new church home, and to attend regularly. Up until now, they have probably not had any choice in the matter, even if they were willing to attend. But have they learned the importance or perhaps better said, the necessity of church attendance? The necessity of gathering with like-minded individuals in corporate worship? This is not just a college problem, though it often begins there, but it is like an unseen epidemic. Untold thousands of Christians never attend church, for the simple reason that they just don't think it is important. Now one reason for this is that they just aren't Christian. 1 John 2:19 makes this clear. "They went out from us, but they were not of us; if they had been of us, they would have continued with us. But they went out, that it might become plain that they all are not of us."

This is a very real reason why young people as well as adults leave the church, but what we are primarily looking at is a lack of education by the church on why attendance is so important. For the moment we are going to give the benefit of the doubt to many college age students who leave the church, and say that they are Christian. If so, then the only reason they don't show up at some type of service is that it just isn't important to them; it holds no place of relevance.

Also to be fair, it isn't always easy to find a decent church out there. Where opinions and conjecture and error are taught instead of doctrine based upon clear teaching of the Bible, there is sure to be danger. Best to stay clear of such places. But for the most part college towns are large enough that surely someone can find a church worth attending, even if it isn't the denomination you grew up in. These two areas we just looked at are very important, and not to be taken lightly, but back to the point of obedience.

Most of us are familiar with the passage in Hebrews 10:24-25, (ESV) "And let us consider how to stir up one another to love and good works, not neglecting to meet together, as is the habit of some, but encouraging one another, and all the more as you see the Day drawing near." The habit of some is to neglect meeting together. It has become a habit, or a routine of life, it seems to not be important. But where else is it that Christians can be stirred up to love and good works, and be encouraged in a world that is hostile to Christianity, if it isn't at the church house? Now something for us all to think about, is are we actually doing this? Are you stirring up others to love and good works, or are you encouraging others? Not in a superficial manner, as is so often the case, but in an actual heartfelt motive for their wellbeing? I hope so, because people see right through superficiality. You need to be in a place where you are being encouraged, but at the same time you are allowed to encourage others. We are to stir one another up to good works like a hive of bees that are agitated. Our love and encouragement is meant to feed off of one another, to stir ourselves up to good works and encouragement. It doesn't happen nearly often enough, but if you have ever been in a church like that, you will know what I am talking about.

But more importantly, this is a command from God. We can never read the bible without foremost realizing that it is a revelation of God's will in how to live our life. Not the idea of an apostle, or some good sounding tradition, but the will of God revealed in the written word. This is directed to that student out there who might think sleeping in after a hard night of extracurricular activities (another area of obedience most are lacking in) is more important than going to church. We have only singled out this one area that you are going to have struggles in, as there are several others worth mentioning, but this one is most critical. Direct yourself back to that quote mentioned earlier, and really meditate on it. "Disobedience often begins at a point where obedience would be easy, but we do not think it important." It is often the neglect of the little things, the easy things that lead us into disobedience, for we just don't think the little things are important. Not that church attendance is a little thing, but if you are already doing it, remember why, and don't stop. Those who are not faithful in the little things rarely are faithful in that which is most important, their soul and its well-being.

This goes without saying that it is applicable to all of us, whether young or old, or all those points in between. It is a faithful saying that no temptation has ever over taken you except those that are common to all, but if you look for it, God always provides a means of escape. But you will have to be obedient and take that means of escape, even if it seems like a small thing. So the next time you feel yourself being drawn to an act of disobedience, consider why you don't think it is important to obey. Meditate on that last sentence, and may it be an encouragement for you, and stir your mind up to obedience. Shalom.

REST, RECREATION, OR WORSHIP?

What is Sunday for? Millions of us go to church each Sunday, presumably and hopefully to worship our Lord and Savior Jesus Christ. But do you ever from time to time contemplate the day, or has it become a routine and ritual you go through every week? Have you ever sat down and just meditated on those words of Jesus which state that man wasn't made for the Sabbath, but the Sabbath was meant for man? What does the Sabbath mean to you?

We are not going to get bogged down on all the issues that can come up, such as Saturday vs. Sunday, and the like, but simply what is the Sabbath for? Is it for rest, recreation, worship, a combination of all three, or do you not even give it a second thought?

This is a subject that has come up occasionally, and while there are other matters of greater concern, we need to remind ourselves of the importance of the Sabbath. What brought this to mind today was the incredibly nice weather we are having at this time of year, and the vast number of people I saw out enjoying a time of recreation on my return home from church. Even in my mind I was thinking today would be a really good time to go out and bike ride, or do something outside while it is nice. After all, church is over, and I have done my duty. Isn't that what the vast majority of our fellow church goers believe? If truth be told, isn't that what we tell ourselves also, or if we don't think it, our actions do? On the one extreme we can run the risk of a ridged legalism and on the other side callousness to the day and almost a sense of antinomianism.

There is a gym I pass by every day, a 24 hour gym I believe, but it seems to be always busy, and today was no exception. And this is what bothered me. Not that there might be Christians in there working out; that is something between them and God, and I will leave my personnel opinion out, but that there is so many lost people out there more concerned with their body, than with their soul. God has given us this one day in which, if we will use the means He has provided, we can enrich our soul. Yet, Christians included, we tend to promote or indulge ourselves in those ways and means which bring pleasure to the body, and leave the soul to languish. If you have ever wondered why your Christian life is not vibrant, perhaps that is the reason. You have become so preoccupied with your physical well-being, that you have left your spiritual muscles as it were to atrophy.

So what are we to use the Sabbath for? Rest, recreation, and worship can all be incorporated into the day, but in all of it, God should be included. For example, I know of a couple who sometimes after worship services go out kayaking, and it is a rest and recreation at the same time; a getting away from the business of everyday life, and they contemplate the nature that God has made and enjoy the fellowship that God has granted them with one another and with Him. And if we can reach those times when we walk hand in hand with our maker in the cool of the day, isn't that just a little taste of what is to come in eternity? Those times don't come nearly often enough, but the Sabbath is an especially good day to remember our creator and what He has created us for. And that is to glorify Him, and to fully enjoy Him forever.

But lest we get caught up in doxology and get off topic, (though our praise to God on this most special of days can hardly be called off topic, and we remember those praises of Paul in various places which cause our hearts to leap in joy, the joy of our salvation, and eternal life in Jesus who loved us and gave Himself for us) how should the Sabbath or rather as it is more frequently called now, the Lord's day to be set apart, to be sanctified? Always I am drawn back to the Westminster confession of faith, and question 117 of the larger catechism.

Q. How is the Sabbath or Lord's Day to be sanctified?

A. The Sabbath or Lord's day is to be sanctified by an holy resting all the day, not only from such works as are at all times sinful, but even from such worldly employments and recreations as are on other days lawful, and making it our delight to spend the whole time (except as much of it as is to be taken up in works of necessity and mercy) in the public and private exercise of God's worship. And, to that end we are to prepare our hearts, and with such foresight, diligence, and moderation, to dispose and seasonably dispatch our worldly business, that we may be the more free and fit for the duties of that day.

Now I realize that many of you may not be familiar with the Westminster confession of faith, and I would encourage you to prayerfully immerse yourself in what it has to say, but it seems to hit the mark here. This answer in how the Lord's Day is to be set apart from all others is not easy in the current culture we live in, but at the end of the day, I think every Christian wants to live this way.

Suspect are those who want to get the worship service over so they can do their own thing; not talking about those works of necessity and mercy, for of necessity some people must work and take care of others. But those suspect we are talking about are those who want the worship service to be over so they can get out to the lake and go fishing, or get to the ball game, or you fill in the blank for your favorite activity.

These are not easy things in all cases to do, as the pleasures of this world continue to gnaw at us even after regeneration, or being born again. There is an activity I enjoy, which I suppose could fall into one of those grey areas, but really is probably sin, that I can only do on Sunday. Now fortunate for me, it is on Sunday and so it is not as serious a temptation. God will provide a way out right? But what if it was on another weekday at a time when other obligations did not attend? We could go off on a tangent here, but think of this, and consider it of all things you do. Is it for the glory of God, or for you? The Sabbath day, do you celebrate it, long for it, desire it in the depths of your heart as a time you get to formally and corporately meet with God? Or is it a day in which to ease your guilty conscience, you have set apart a few hours in which you think you have satisfied God, by attending church services? Eternal destinations are revealed in that answer my friend.

I am starting to ramble and lest I totally lose focus, I want to encourage all of my brothers and sisters in Christ who (including myself) sometimes struggle in setting apart the Sabbath day. Setting the day apart in such a way that it really is different than all the others, and it goes a long way in remembering who we are.

And so with all my rambling and possible confusion, I want to leave you with two verses which help me a lot in this issue and with others as well. Meditate on them well, and may the peace of God be with you all. Shalom.

1Peter 4:3 (NET) "For the time that has passed was sufficient for you to do what the non-Christians desire. You lived then in debauchery, evil desires, drunkenness, carousing, drinking bouts, and wanton idolatries."

Galatians2:20 (KJV) "I am crucified with Christ; nevertheless I live; yet not I but Christ liveth in me; and the life I now live in the flesh I live by the faith of the Son of God who loved me and gave himself for me."

WE HAVE BEEN BORN AGAIN; LIVE LIKE IT AND REMEMBER THE SABBATH TO KEEP IT HOLY

A DILEMNA WITH TERRIBLE CONSEQUENCES

As we begin a New Year, it would do well to consider what our life is about. What is your purpose, and what are you here for. Are you just a bunch of random atoms that after billions of years somehow got together and formed the human race? It is almost absurd to think so, yet many people think this is what happened. Or perhaps there was just nothingness; no atoms or quarks or anything, just nothingness. Then nothing created everything. Now this is even more absurd then the previous idea, but there are some who adhere to this view of how everything came about. We could enumerate several more ideas, but that is not the point of this post. The point is that the majority of the human race never considers these questions, but blindly follows what they are told, regardless of how ridiculous it might sound.

Now as Christians, we believe that an eternal, self-existing being that we call God, created everything out of nothing, by the word of His power. And, we are accused many times of the same thing; of blindly following what we are told, regardless of how ridiculous it might sound. Now there are many arguments for the existence of God, very good arguments in fact, so it isn't ridiculous, but quite credible. It also isn't a very good idea to blindly follow what someone says, or believe them when it comes to religious ideas or beliefs, unless they can back them up; this is where apologetics comes in.

Again, as Christians, we know that the only authority we have, or what must have the final say, is the bible. If we start relying on traditions of men, or those in funny hats who usurp the authority of God, as if they were God, we are going to end up in error. We also know that the bible is spiritually discerned, and so there is that element of unbelief that will always exist in the minds of men, as to its authority to govern their life. But that isn't always our biggest obstacles when it comes to sharing our faith; the biggest obstacle is apathy. Apathy is probably not the right word, but as Blaise Pascal says, they are tranquil in their ignorance; they don't know and don't want to know.

How often is it that we speak to individuals of the eternal destiny that awaits each one of us when we die? To say it more bluntly, we confront them with heaven and hell, and the what fors and what nots (the gospel) and they politely say they respect our right to have that opinion, but they decline to acquiesce. Then off they go and never give it anymore consideration. We might not ever proclaim the gospel to them again, but there might be something we are overlooking, and that is to confront them with a greater problem, (if there is such a thing) and that is their unwillingness to see if our claims have any merit.

If we are wrong, then there is a sense in which we could say no harm no foul, but if we are right, it is a dilemma with terrible consequences. It is this which we must also get them to consider. I am going to be giving several quotes, all by Blaise Pascal in the work Penses, but I want you to consider them not only for your own life, but when we speak with others about Jesus and eternity.

"It is beyond doubt that this life's duration is but an instant, that the state of death is eternal, whatever its nature may be." There are "those who live without reflecting about their final end of life, who, thoughtless and unworried, follow wherever their inclinations and pleasures take them, as if they could abolish eternity by keeping their minds off of it."

He goes on to say that though we know that eternity exists and that death must be a starting place, and whether we would admit it or not, death threatens us at every moment, we should be concerned about what is coming up. People do not know whether they will be annihilated or "miserable in eternity."

And paraphrasing what he continues on to say here, most people do not think it is worth considering whether or not we are full of it, or there is a foundation of truth to what we say. They refuse to look at the proofs which are right in front of them, and choose to wait until death to test the veracity of our proclamations. But mankind is satisfied and complacent to remain in this state of imbecility and often brag about their superior intellect in the matter when they have done no serious searching as to the truth.

"Can we seriously think of the importance of this matter without being horrified by such outrageous behavior? This tranquility in that ignorance is monstrous and we must make those who spend their lives in this way feel the outrageousness and stupidity of it by pointing it out to them, so they are overcome by the recognition of their folly."

This is something which we must overcome when we proclaim the gospel. We must also make people understand that there is no such thing as sitting on a fence; you are either on one side or the other. It is much like what Jesus tells us in John 3:18. "He who believes in Him (Jesus) is not condemned; but he who does not believe is condemned already, because he has not believed in the name of the only begotten Son of God." There is no middle ground here; you are either condemned or not, and those who refuse to believe are condemned already, and there is an eternity of misery awaiting them.

So as we begin this New Year, let us endeavor to proclaim the gospel with a greater eagerness and a greater zeal, knowing that eternity is at stake, and as we do so let us exhort those with whom we speak, to consider eternity and the choice they have made. They have already made a choice whether they know so or not, and one of our duties is to actually get them to leave a state of ignorance and know what choice they have made. If they have not chosen Christ as Savior, do they really, and I mean really know the consequences of not having a Savior? Make them think about it, and not be satisfied in remaining in an ignorant stupor. And as always we must prayerfully ask that God would change their hearts and minds, for if he had not done so with us, we would be in that same dilemma of terrible consequences that they are in.

For those of you interested in something to keep your mind occupied for a few minutes, I would encourage you to read Pascal's wager. Though I don't agree with everything he has written, he does make you think. So until we meet again, may the Lord bless you and keep you, and may His face shine upon you. Shalom.

EVANGELISM: ARE YOU PARTICIPATING OR PRETENDING?

"The love of God is not here for us to applaud, it is here for us to apply."-M.L. Jones

While searching for a phone number this morning (you would think by now I would store them in my phone) I ran across some more notes and decided to use them for a post today. In a moment there will be five quotes taken from J.I. Packer's introduction to Richard Baxter's book the Reformed Pastor available from the Banner of Truth Trust.

"Evangelism is an expression of Christian love."

"Any Christian who seriously thinks that without Christ men are lost and who seriously loves his neighbor, will not be able to rest for the thought that all around him people are going to hell."

"A Christian who truly believes this will deem it his duty to give himself wholly to converting others as his prime task above all others in this life."

"Any Christian who fails to behave this way in life undermines the credibility of his faith."

"If you can't take it seriously as the priority for your own life, why should anyone else take it seriously as a guide for theirs?"

Now I want you to look over these quotes again, especially the second one, and then ask yourself honestly whether or not you really love your neighbor. If we are honest with one another, we are going to find that most of us fail to take the eternal well-being of our neighbor seriously. And by neighbor, we are talking about those we come into contact with on a regular basis, whether that is the guy living next door or the person we work with, or even the relative we see occasionally. If evangelism is an expression of Christian love, then not evangelizing must be the opposite of love. The opposite of love is not necessarily hate, but apathy. Are you apathetic to the plight of those you come into contact with? Isn't that in a way the apex of hatred? And if it is even possible for you to say that evangelism is not an expression of love, then what is its purpose? Is not evangelism's whole purpose in driving or informing others of that one whose whole life was a demonstration of the greatest love for mankind? And that love was demonstrated by his life being a ransom to deliver us from the wrath of God against sinners. Now most of you know I am speaking about Jesus, but the deliverance he gives is not to all, but only to those who believe. Romans 10 speaks to this when it say that "if you confess with your mouth the Lord Jesus and believe in your heart that God has raised Him from the dead, you will be saved." And, "whoever calls on the name of the Lord shall be saved." But, "how shall they believe in Him of whom they have not heard?" "So then faith comes by hearing and hearing by the word of God."

So if those who say they are Christians are not evangelizing in some way or another how is it that the love of God is demonstrated in them? At the very beginning of this post there is a quote by Martyn Lloyd-Jones which is appropriate for what we are looking at, so let's look at it again. "The love of God is not here for us to applaud, it is here for us to apply." If your love of God is just an academic proposal that you give an assent to and is not reflected in an actual obedience of love, is it right to call it Christianity?

How many of us are living lives that are far short of what they should be, considering the gift of salvation that we have received? The two greatest commandments of loving God and neighbor are practiced at worship but it has a hard time expressing itself the rest of the week. And sadly what passes for Christianity these days, especially if you look online, has little to do with how it is portrayed to us in the Bible. In Christ we are not only free from the guilt of sin, but from the penalty of sin and the power of sin. This doesn't mean we don't trip now and then, but it no longer has any dominion over our life. And if that isn't enough, we look forward to that resurrection and the time when eternity will be spent in a place absent of any sin or the consequences of sin; heaven. But we know the alternative as well, and if like that one quote says, if we truly believe that men without Christ are lost to an eternity in hell, we will do whatever it takes to make them aware of their plight.

And at the end of the day, that is all we can do or are responsible to do. Only God can save someone, and we cannot force someone to believe. Our duty is to proclaim to them the gospel, repeatedly if need be, but after that leave the results to God. How well are you doing that? Hopefully better than I seem to do on most days, but consider your salvation and what it is worth. And if we all believe that all the riches in the world cannot equal the value of even one soul, then no cost will seem too difficult in evangelism. Think on these things and how they relate to your life, and until next time, Shalom.

FAVORITE PSALMS AND MAN'S ENMITY

Sometimes headings are not necessarily a good indication of the topic of a post, but when we are done, perhaps you will see how it fits. 1,37,49,50,73,100,119,137,148,150, and 65 are my favorite psalms for various reasons. Not that they are not all good and useful, but each one of us has those which have particular significance for one reason or another. Did you know you can even analyze someone by this means? Not that it is important, but personally I find those trinkets of information interesting. But the reason we or I bring this up, is that I have been impatiently waiting for someone to speak on psalm 65 for several weeks now. I had intended on writing on this psalm a while back and when I heard this individual was going to speak on it decided not to. Sometimes he might read this post and I would have felt bad if there were any feeling of encroachment on my part, so I decided to leave it alone. Perhaps another time we will look at it in more detail. But there is one verse that we are going to look at in combination with another verse in Psalm 49, which we can relate to man's enmity against God. At least that is the plan if we can do it in the limited space we have allotted ourselves.

V. 4 of psalm 65 starts out, "Blessed is the one you chose and bring near to dwell in your courts!" Then in Psalm 49:15 we read, "But God will redeem my soul from the power of Sheol, for he will receive me." Instead of Sheol, some versions read grave which for most of us is easier to understand. But what is clear is that this is a work of God, not something we are doing for ourselves. We may have looked at this before, but in vs. 7-9 of chap. 49 we see that no one can ransom or redeem another, or even their own life. The price of redemption is costly and there is no amount of money that will suffice; God's righteousness cannot be bought or purchased. It is a gift given to those whom he chooses; it is he that redeems us.

Now we are not going to go into all the theological jargon that some think is a necessity to know (though it does enrich the Christian walk), but the gospel boils down simply to that man is a sinner and God has provided salvation by faith in Jesus Christ. It is written, believe on the Lord Jesus Christ and you will be saved; Saved from the wrath of God upon all who are ungodly and walk in sin. Of course those who believe will turn from their former ways and seek to live holy lives, and be in obedience to the commands of God, but why would anyone desire to endure the wrath of God? Those who will not repent and believe are in essence doing that very thing. Towards the end of chapter 1 in Romans we have a list of those manifestations of sin that some indulge themselves in, and it makes it very clear that they know it is wrong. They are completely aware that though God has decreed that those who practice such things deserve death, they not only do them, but approve of those who do. All you have to do is turn on the news or the internet, and see this in full blown action. And yet, these people have no excuse for they are fully aware of the criminality of their actions before God, and don't care; they have no fear of God. In a very real sense their sin against the salvation of God is greater than that of Adam and Eve's when mankind first fell, for they are purposefully and willfully, with eyes wide open, declaring their enmity. They spurn the love of God, proving by their actions that they would rather spend eternity enduring the wrath of God, than turning from the temporary pleasures of sin, if they are even finding them pleasurable. Or, it could be that they just think God is a liar and will not do as he has threatened.

This describes many of you reading this post. You have heard the gospel of salvation by faith in Christ, but refuse to make a decision, which is really a decision of refusal. There is not a third choice, but you keep thinking that maybe there is, or that your attempt to be good is that third choice. What is it they say, but the road to hell is paved with good intentions. YOUR goodness is irrelevant, for there is none who are good and have been perfect except for Jesus Christ the Son of God. It is his righteousness and atoning death and then resurrection that by faith is imputed to you, but on your own there is no hope. Again, some of you know this, but don't care, and this is further evidence of your enmity against God. But I want you to consider something and though I am not going to go into great detail, listen carefully. (If you can find it we have written somewhat more thoroughly on this in the past.) You believe there is a God, though you hate him, but you don't fear him. But even the devils believe there is a God, and they tremble. They know God's power and righteousness and shake in fear before him and at the thought of him; do you?

When a third of the angels rebelled against God and left their proper domain, do you think they understood the ramifications of what they were doing? Having an intimate knowledge of God, his power, his omniscience, his omnipotence and all his other attributes, why do you think they rebelled? They became enemies of God, just as you are, but with one big difference. There is no salvation available for them. Their destiny is an eternity enduring the wrath of God, and not only do they know it, they have known it for a very long time. Make no mistake about it, their knowledge of theology if you want to say it that way, is impeccable. There are no disputations over those things we argue about, many of which are useless wranglings by the way, and if you could hear them speak, you might be enthralled at their comprehension of religious things. But despite all this they still hate God, for they are destined for that bleak eternity and they dread the day of final judgement. This is one of the reasons they hate mankind, in that God HAS provided us a means of deliverance; we have the possibility of salvation. We have been created in the image of God, not them, and God loves us in a way which is different, in that he provides reconciliation.

There is more that could be said on this subject, but for now let us focus on you. You are not an angel or a devil, even if you act like one, and have a hatred for God like they do. As such, you have the opportunity to choose Christ as your Savior. But if you will not, isn't that an even greater manifestation of enmity against God than the devils have? Knowing the wrath of God against all unrighteousness and having the opportunity to repent and yet not doing so, is the greatest of sins and in the millennia of ages to come you will begin to understand that, though I am certain you will understand it in the first five minutes, and with a perfect understanding that there is no end. If this doesn't make you tremble, then nothing will, until you stand before the judgement seat of Christ, and then every knee will bow; either in reverence or in fear.

Today's post really should have been split up into several parts in order that clarity might be given to some of you who are so steeped in the affairs of the days we live in that your mind has become mush. Can you not see the hatred and division that certain groups out there are stirring up? Can you not see the true motivations that are behind their rhetoric? It has nothing to do with the outward appearances, but it is just an outpouring of the evil that is within all men's hearts. It is an evil that is at enmity with God and man, and the only thing restraining it from getting worse is the common grace of the Holy Spirit. But perhaps we are in those last times where the restraints are lifted off, and all will see the evil that lurks in each one of our hearts.

And yet even now, God is calling out to some and they are hearing his voice that today is the day of salvation; believe in the Lord Jesus Christ and you will be saved. There is still hope while there is breath in your lungs to be reconciled to God by faith in Christ. Today is the day to choose life.

Blessed are those whom God chooses to bring near to dwell in his courts. Shalom.

RESOLUTION 2021

As most of you are aware if you are receiving this, every year I send out a little encouraging resolution concerning the coming year. Last year we concentrated on number 48 of Jonathan Edwards resolutions, and we ended it all with this paragraph:

"As we start a new year, let us renew our efforts to walk more Christ like, loving our neighbors as ourselves and God with our whole being. Let us not be quite so concerned about the trivial things of everyday life, such as stock markets and government elections and scandals and media madness, but let us concentrate on the souls of men and eternity. In the end, this is what matters, so in that respect, let us set our affection on things above, for our life as it concerns worldly things is over. And also to this end, we must proclaim the gospel to all creatures, for eternity is at stake. If we would just resolve to remember that there is an eternity, much of this would fall into place."

Now we must admit that this year has been anything but trivial. We have had a heavy dose of market fluctuations, election scandals and rumors, and media madness seems to have reached a new level. But to top it all off, we had ourselves the pandemic of COVID-19 to deal with. It has changed our world in so many ways, that it might take years to realize the full ramifications of what has taken place, and continues to take place. The way we go about our daily lives has changed; more so for some than for others. So it almost seems careless, or perhaps indifferent, to call this pandemic trivial, but ask yourself how it fits into the eternality of all things? Is it worth fretting over?

There are other questions which each of us may have to answer soon, such as how we are going to view the vaccine which will be available to us in the very near future. If, and it is a big (?) if, what is going to be our stance on mandatory vaccinations, or even forced vaccinations? There is a very good likelihood that 2021 may be just as disruptive or more so than 2020. How are we going to respond to government edicts that may not be based on law, but expediency?

I have no reason to think otherwise, but that all of those to whom I am writing are Christian. So what is the Christian response to these and other questions that may arise and have arisen over the past year? Unfortunately the biblical response is usually the one we tend to ignore, and look for those passages which seem to agree with our natural human response. These are many times quite opposed to one another, and to top it all off, we often disagree with one another what it is that the biblical response should be. I will not even try to answer that one, but I want to look at three resolutions that might help you in the coming year. And while we briefly look at them, notice how highly individualistic they are. Sometimes if we would endeavor to fix ourselves, or allow the Holy Spirit to work in us, instead of being worried about what the other guy is doing or thinking, we would be better off. You can't help remembering what Jesus told Peter when Peter asked Jesus about John. Do you remember the response? Jesus told Peter that if John remained until he returned, "What is that to you? You follow me." So again, as we look at these resolutions, see if they are applicable to you and if so, great, but if not, that is okay too. We will again be looking at Jonathan Edwards's resolution, numbers 55, 56, and 57, and in reverse order.

#57, Resolved when I fear misfortunes and adversity, to examine whether I have done my duty, and resolve to do it, and let the event be just as Providence orders it. I will as far as I can, be concerned about nothing but my duty and my sin."

My duty and my sin. I cannot speak for anyone but myself, but isn't it a whole lot easier to look at the other guy's duty and sin? I measure up pretty well if I do that, or so we think, but it is easy to forget that God doesn't grade on a curve. My obedience or lack thereof, of the word of God, is something He only is able to judge, not you or myself. But in saying that, we also forget that we can never measure up to the perfection that is required, and that our obedience if found in the obedience of Christ. We can never ever forget this. My obedience or your obedience has nothing to do with the righteous obedience that God requires, but our faith in Christ; His obedience imputed unto us. Nevertheless, it is my duty to be about the things of God and especially as to the mortification or killing of sin; another topic for another day, but a necessity if we are to grow into the likeness of Christ. But in the coming year, let us concentrate on doing our duty to God and our neighbor, and to the mortification of sin in our minds and bodies, and let such things as COVID-19 and elections and such take their proper place as the things of this world.

"I have been crucified with Christ. It is no longer I who live, but Christ who lives in me. And the life I now live in the flesh I live by faith in the Son of God, who loved me and gave Himself for me." Galatians 2:20.

#56, "Never to give over, nor in the least to slacken, my fight with my corruptions, however unsuccessful I may be."

We are in a fight people, and in some ways it is so subtle, that we don't know it. Like the frog put into a kettle of water which is slowly heated, we are for the most part oblivious to our sin. Now and then there may be some discomfort when the Holy Spirit slaps you alongside the head, but is it enough to wake you up out of your slumber? Now the outward manifestations of sin are in many respects, quite pleasurable, but they have their birth in inward corruptions. Now for the Christian, these inward corruptions are the remnants of that sinful nature we were born with, but they in fact have been crucified with Christ. We could really get into a lot of stuff here, but the bottom line is that we are not just in a fight, but a war. We are always going to stumble in one way or another, but we must never give up. But it is also another reason to give God the glory for what He has done in our salvation.

"So I find it to be a law that when I want to do right, evil lies close at hand. For I delight in the law of God, in my inner being, but I see in my members another law waging war against the law of my mind and making me captive to the law of sin that dwells in my members. Wretched man that I am! Who will deliver me from this body of death? Thanks be to God through Jesus Christ our Lord! So then I myself serve the law of God with my mind, but with my flesh I serve the law of sin." Romans 7:21-25. (ESV)

We have all been there haven't we? We know what our duty is, and we desire to do it, and to refrain from sin, but for one reason or another, we just can't do it. Without getting off on a tangent, can you not see this war within yourself? I can't speak for you, but sometimes I want to cry out, WHO WILL DELIVER ME? And, I can do nothing but humble myself before God and give Him thanks for Christ Jesus our Lord who has saved us from our sin. When I think upon these things, it is easy to see with what ease Paul the apostle goes into such doxologies as he does, and the only wonder is that he ever stops, and the only reason he ever stops, is that at a certain point, human words can never express the deep love and gratitude that we have for our Savior. It is to the thanksgiving and glory of the praise of His unsearchable grace, which no mere words can convey. Which gives us a miniscule glimpse and taste of heaven.

#55, "Resolved, to endeavor, to my utmost, so to act, as I can think I should do, if I had already seen the happiness of heaven and hell torments."

It is easy to go in many directions here, but I want to spend just a moment on evangelism. Perhaps we have gotten a glimpse of heaven when we see the love of God towards us in the face of Jesus, and what He has done for us, but do you ever take a glimpse into that chasm of dark hopelessness, that fiery torment of eternal damnation which we give the name hell? It would do you all well to spend a few minutes in that darkness, that darkness which can be felt, those eternal chains of darkness. Much has been written on hell and its torments, some fanciful, some real, but it is truly said that above the gates of hell, it is written, ABANDON ALL HOPE YE WHICH ENTER HERE.

There are many questions on the doctrine of hell these days, but I truly believe if you will read Luke 16, it will give a solid discourse on it. But what I want you to do, if you have never done it, is to place yourself there. Make no mistake, that was your destined end had not the grace of God, for His own good pleasure rescued you. Do you ever contemplate what that would be like? Disregard for a moment the physical torments which you are or would have had to endure, but think of the mental anguish. Most of us will never live past 70 or 80 years, but imagine what it would be like to live in isolation for thousands of years. Likely this would be in total darkness, or who knows, in the blindingly fiery of the glory of God. It is too weighty to imagine the glory of God, for who can look upon Him and live, but darkness? I want you to use your imagination here, and think what it might be like? Step into the abyss that is hell if you can, and then, if sanity remains, can you wish anyone there? Only a devil would say so. Love your enemies, if perhaps that through your love, Christ might save them. This is but a feathery touch upon what it means to look into the chasm of hell, and the glorious bliss which no human words can describe that is the abode of heaven.

In closing, think on these three resolutions. Do they mean anything to you at all, assuming you have read through this article? And in the coming minutes, hours days, years, and yes, eternity, do they touch your heart? Concerning your sin and duty, are you endeavoring to fight the war which is raging inside of you? And in light of eternity are you warning those who might fall? Not fall into sin, for all have sinned, but that fall into the abyss of hell. Only by faith in Christ can one obtain salvation. Think on these things during the upcoming year.

Now may the Lord bless you and keep you, May the Lord make His face to shine upon you and be gracious to you, and may the Lord lift up his countenance upon you and give you peace. Until we meet, Shalom.

FOUR POSTS CONCERNING COVID

Early in 2020, before covid became an epidemic, we were kicked off of Facebook, and what few articles we did after that were sent via e-mail. As stated in the introduction, our web site and blog never did that well, but being removed from Facebook was a depressing death blow. As such, only a handful of people have seen the remaining posts and articles in this book. Hopefully the reader will find them edifying, and God will in some way be glorified. The next four posts are more directly related to covid, and though several years have passed, I feel as if they are as applicable today as when they were first written.

PRESUMPTION OR UNBELIEF?

There is a story in the Old Testament which those of you who are Christian are quite familiar with, and that is the account of Joshua and Caleb. If you are not acquainted with it, I must ask you why not, but for those who are not familiar with it, I will give the cliff notes. God had miraculously delivered the Israelites from their slave masters in Egypt, and had brought them to a land which they were to take possession of. Twelve spies were sent in to check it out, and they came back with a report that indeed the land was fruitful, but the people that lived in it were large and they convinced the people that to go in would be foolhardy; but not so Caleb and Joshua. They affirmed that if the Lord was with them, as He had demonstrated to them in the past in many ways and miracles, then to not advance would be rebellion against the Lord. You can read the whole story in the book of Numbers if you are not familiar with it, but the end result was that only two people that were over the age of twenty would enter this Promised Land, and that was Caleb and Joshua; everyone else died in the wilderness in a wandering that lasted forty years. They died and were forsaken for their unbelief in the promises of God.

How many of us in this day and age are living lives of fear and rejection simply because we do not belief the promises of God? Now I know many who turn to Psalm 91 in days such as we are living in currently, but for the most part I see them taking comfort in reading it, but not living it. We say we believe the word of God, and we have professed saving faith in Jesus Christ, but we don't live it. Read Psalm 91 for yourself and ask if you believe it or not. There are other such passages in the Bible, but this is just the one that first came to mind.

Now whenever I read this Psalm, I cannot help but thinking of Mother Teresa who spent her life working among the lepers in Calcutta. It is very rare that we see such faith displayed, and though I have never read any of her biographies, we can be assured that she believed in the promises of God. This brings us to our dilemma at this present time.

How many of us have isolated ourselves from others because we are fearful of getting this virus that is going around? Did you isolate yourself during the last crisis and are you going to isolate during the next one? There are so many scenarios and what ifs, that it is pointless to try and answer them all, but have you shut down your life because you are afraid? Some of us are in situations where we could continue to work, but to do so would expose us to the public, and IF we contracted the virus, we could expose others to the risk. What is the prudent and most expedient thing to do? If you can work from home or take vacation time, or have funds to ride this out, then the question may not dwell in your mind as much as it does in those who can't.

As Christians, we are to be model citizens, and obey those governmental edicts to disassociate ourselves temporarily for the good of society. To not do so and possibly infect others would not be very neighborly would it? The Westminster confession of Faith clarifies that the commands we have are twofold. When it says we are not to murder, it includes the corollary that we are to do all that is in our power to do that which tends to the wellbeing or life of another. Purposefully putting another in harm's way is not in accordance with keeping this commandment. But at what point do we get on with life and say "My God, in Him will I trust."?

Are we going to cower in fear every time the world gets its panties in a wad? This is a time where we can encourage others and help those when we have an opportunity to do so, but not if we are in hiding. Where would the church be today if Peter and John had complied with the wishes of the rulers, and hid themselves? Now hopefully this crisis we are going through will end quickly, but it is doubtful that everything will return to normal. But in what may ensue, are we going to take our marching orders from this world system, or trust in God?

So my dilemma as well as many others, is that we trust that we can go about our daily business and not get sick. To not go about our daily business (if we can do so) is a lack of trust in God's providence. Yet, at what point are we being presumptuous?

When Jesus was tempted by Satan in the desert, Satan used the very psalm we referenced earlier. The devil took Jesus and set him on the pinnacle of the temple and said to him "If you are the Son of God, throw yourself down. For it is written: 'He shall give His angels charge over you and in their hands they shall bear you up, lest you dash your foot against a stone.'"

And this is the part we must concern ourselves with and it is Jesus' reply. "It is written again, you shall not test the Lord your God." So at what point are we being presumptuous and testing God, and at what point is it unbelief in the promises of God? If we defy gravity and jump off a cliff thinking God is going to save us, we are going beyond presumption and the testing of God, and being plain stupid. But is isolating ourselves from possible contamination in the same category? Some would say yes, and to expose ourselves is just plain stupid. But are we not different than those in this world system? Are not the promises of God to His people as applicable today as in the day they were written? If not, where is our hope?

Personally, for myself, I think it is an act of unbelief on our part, and we are no different than the hundreds of thousands who died in the desert, and only two entered the Promised Land. But, to be even more honest, I could be wrong. I waver between presumption and unbelief. So if anyone is capable of answering this in a biblical way, (I will also listen to opinion) let me know. In the meantime, perhaps prayer and fasting will be our answer. Until we meet again, Shalom.

HE STAGGERED NOT

As mentioned Wednesday, we are going to look at a biblical answer concerning our response to the promises of God. Previously in a post on presumption and unbelief which somewhat concerned our response during this pandemic of the virus, and the fear it has generated, I posed this question or challenge, "I waver between presumption and unbelief. So if anyone is capable of answering this in a biblical way, (I will also listen to opinion) let me know."

Now it is not the intention to say that we ignore this virus, far from it, and it is only prudent that we use alternate methods of worship, such as the internet during this turbulent time. I do believe many have approached it not only in a presumptuous way, but others in a way of unbelief. Now we had looked at Psalm 91, and we will bring it into context later, however, the way in which we respond to all the promises of God, is what we are going to briefly look at. Also, this is meant to be very personal; in other words, don't apply it to the church as a whole, or each individual congregation, but as it directly concerns you personally. You might not like what you find.

"He staggered not at the promise of God through unbelief." Romans 4:20.

Now it is not possible in a post such as this to give all the details of the context, or the history of Abraham, which is the one being spoken of that did not stagger. Some of you may not be familiar with the life of Abraham, but in a nutshell, God had promised him that he would be the father of many nations, though when the promise was given he was childless. If you will read Romans 4 it will help, but v.19 says "And being not weak in faith he considered not his own body now dead, when he was about a hundred years old, neither yet the deadness of Sarah's womb." In other words, physically speaking they were past the age of having children, yet Abraham was fully persuaded that what God had promised he was also able to perform, and therefore did not stagger at the promise of God through unbelief.

Again, if you are not familiar with the life of Abraham, and the promises given to him and his SEED, it would do you good to take up a concordance and read those passages in the bible dealing with Abraham. I can understand that those who are not churched or young believers may be unfamiliar with all this, but if there is anyone out there who has been a Christian for any length of time and does not know this, ask yourself why not? Perhaps you live in a land with few bibles and resources, but otherwise someone is neglecting their duties. It is much easier to speak on generic social issues then it is on sin, repentance and redemption. But we are really straying here, so let us get back to considering our response to the promises of God.

Sometimes this word stagger is in some versions waver, but it has the idea of judging or discriminating, perhaps taking all factors into consideration. But in the very act of weighing the different factors involved in a promise of God, there is that element of unbelief which says that maybe this promise is not real. To make it clear, we are not talking about the conditions of the promise, but obstacles. Abraham could have very easily looked at the obstacles of his and Sarah's old age and doubted that they could have any children, but he didn't waver or doubt the promise of God; there was no unbelief. "All staggering at the promises of God is from unbelief."-J.O.

But some promises seem to be conditional, such as we saw in Psalm 91. In v.1 it states that he who dwells in the secret place of the Most High shall abide under the shadow of the Almighty. In v.14 we have God speaking "Because he has set his love upon Me, therefore I will deliver him." If we do not set our love upon God and dwell in the secret place of the Most High, we should not expect that this psalm is speaking to us. But if this does describe us, then to doubt or stagger at this promise is none other than unbelief. Now we are prone to think of many reasons besides unbelief concerning the promises of God, such as it is for someone else or for a different time frame. Or maybe that there is a bit of presumption upon taking the promise to ourselves, but in all these cases it is unbelief in what God has said. And, is that not to call God a liar? Wasn't that one of the serpent's arguments in the Garden of Eden; has God really said...? Think about that the next time you are wavering over what God has declared in His word.

When men make promises they may break them, and whether or not this is on purpose or circumstances, we know that it happens. But the stability of a promise depends on the qualifications of the promiser, and if God cannot lie, than any deviation of our thinking from the promise is unbelief in the character of God. This is why those who do not believe the gospel are in essence calling God a liar by their unbelief and disobedience. It is a very dangerous place to be. It is not just unbelievers who are in this predicament, but how many Christians are in a state of unbelief as it relates to the promises of God? How is it we entrust our souls through faith to the promise of God, and yet will not trust Him in much lesser things? Search yourself on that one.

"Faith in the promises and the accomplishment of the promise are inseparable." –J.O.

At the end of this article I will give you the reference for which most of this came from today, but as I was reading it through, the name it and claim it people kept popping into my head. Sometimes it is called the prosperity gospel, but one of the things they always say when things don't work out, is that your faith wasn't strong enough. You would have been healed of that cancer with just a little more faith; we have all heard such stories, so how do we reconcile that with a promise of God?

We must beware of taking the things which belong to God and twisting them to our own carnal advantage. We have a perfect example of this in James 4:2-3. "You do not have because you do not ask. You ask and do not receive because you ask amiss that you may spend it on your pleasures." God is not going to give you a million dollars so you can go buy a party boat and spend your weekends at the lake. We may have a faith which moves mountains and have no doubt whatsoever when it comes to the promises of God, but if it is to satisfy worldly desires; it comes from a heart of evil. We could continue in the passage we looked at in James, and see that friendship with the world is enmity with God. If your desire is to be a friend of this world, then it is also your desire to be an enemy of God. We cannot twist the promises of God into something they were not meant to be.

However, we are to believe the promises as they were given. When we are told that He will never leave us or forsake us (those who are believers) it is a promise we can take comfort in. Any staggering at this promise is from a heart of unbelief and grieves, provokes and dishonors God. And so it is with all the promises. When we presume that a promise might not be for us, it is a wavering, probably from unbelief.

Now how you choose to view all this in light of our current situation as concerning this virus is up to you. Personally it brings great comfort in knowing that I do not need to be anxious about those things in which I have no control over. How this works out practically will vary according to each of our predicaments, but it should be in light of the promises of God, not in the fear of the unknown which the world is currently living in. With that being said, there are two great promises of God which millions through unbelief hazard themselves. The first promise is that all who sin (and all are sinners) will die not only physically and spiritually, but eternally enduring the wrath of God for their unbelief. Also, that the wrath of God is for the punishment of their sin, and that He has provided a way of escape, and that is by faith in the atoning work of His Son Jesus, dying on a cross in our place. And the great second promise which we have is that God so loved the world that He gave his only begotten son that whosoever would believe on him would not perish but have eternal life. DO NOT STAGGER.

Some of these days' thoughts were incomplete, and though it might be possible over several days to expand on them, we will not do so unless requested. However, much of the material today came from thoughts on a sermon by John Owen entitled The Steadfastness of the Promises, and the Sinfulness of Staggering. It goes into much greater detail and clarity and would be beneficial to any who wonder about such things. It can be found on the internet at http://www.godrules.net/library/owen/131-295owen_h11.htm There are two or three of you who know me and if you call me you can come over and read and discuss it.

These days are difficult as we transition into a new way of life, but endurable as we look into all the promises of God that He has in store for us. Help those you can and pray for those you can't, and until we meet again, Shalom.

TO VAX OR NOT TO VAX

"To be or not to be: That is the question..." Now I am not a rabid fan of Shakespeare, in fact I am not very studious in his works at all, but strangely, I do like what I have read or heard from him. And though I am not real familiar with Hamlet, the play from which this quote comes from, it is a question which all persons of even a modicum of intelligence have asked themselves. What does it mean to BE or exist as a living being; what is the purpose? And if you find an answer, does not the futility of life lead you to the next obvious question; why go on or NOT TO BE?

The Christian (after all if we are writing as The Christian Disciple that will be our focus) has the only answer, and that is that great Westminster confession of faith reply, "The chief end (or purpose) of man is to glorify God and enjoy Him forever." It is all about God; not you. This goes contrary to everything in our nature and everything we have been taught from the earliest days of our recollection.

> To be, or not to be, that is the question:
>
> Whether 'tis nobler in the mind to suffer
>
> The slings and arrows of outrageous fortune,
>
> Or to take arms against a sea of troubles
>
> And by opposing end them. To die—to sleep,
>
> No more; and by a sleep to say we end
>
> The heart-ache and the thousand natural shocks
>
> That flesh is heir to: 'tis a consummation
>
> Devoutly to be wish'd. To die, to sleep;

To sleep, perchance to dream—ay, there's the rub:

For in that sleep of death what dreams may come,

When we have shuffled off this mortal coil,

Must give us pause—there's the respect

That makes calamity of so long life.

For who would bear the whips and scorns of time,

Th'oppressor's wrong, the proud man's contumely,

The pangs of dispriz'd love, the law's delay,

The insolence of office, and the spurns

That patient merit of th'unworthy takes,

When he himself might his quietus make

With a bare bodkin? Who would fardels bear,

To grunt and sweat under a weary life,

But that the dread of something after death,

The undiscovere'd country, from whose bourn

No traveller returns, puzzles the will,

And makes us rather bear those ills we have

Than fly to others that we know not of?

Thus conscience doth make cowards of us all,

And thus the native hue of resolution

Is sicklied o'er with the pale cast of thought,

And enterprises of great pith and moment

With this regard their currents turn awry

And lose the name of action.

"The undiscovered country, from whose bourn no traveler returns puzzles the will." There is a certain apprehension about what comes after death, and it scares us. Now if I didn't know better I would think this was copied right out of the book of Ecclesiastes. Without purpose in life there is a certain futility in going on; after all as Solomon says, it is all vanity, a striving after the wind. So why is it people do everything in their power to live just a little bit longer? Our conscience does make us cowards, and for those individuals in the world who are not believers in the Lord Jesus Christ, there is a true dread of something after death. Why?

If natural morality teaches us anything, it teaches that there are three great universal truths which each person believes. 1) That there is a God or deity, a being whom we are responsible to. 2) That freedom is a universal right for all men, and 3) that we are destined to immortality. Now how aware each person is of these great truths, and the ramifications it has for the way we live our life, is quite varied. Most people never give it a second thought, but it is always there, somewhere in their consciousness, just waiting to be explored. We do not have time to expand on this now, but if truth be told, it is much more comfortable to suppress these thoughts into the depths of our being rather than face the fact that we are not autonomous, and we exist for a purpose.

Admittedly, many gods and deities have been created by the imaginations of man and devils, but there is only One God and it is He that has created us in his image for his glory and for his good pleasure. It is he that reveals himself to mankind, not something we make up to appease our guilty conscience. I think Hebrews 1 says it best. "God who at various times and in various ways spoke in time past to the fathers by the prophets, has in these last days spoken to us by his Son."

We have all this recorded for us in the bible, and now is not the place for apologetics, but the hard truth of the matter is that we exist for God. Something William Plumer said has always stuck in my mind, and that is "never was the human being born that did not make some impression on the world." God created us for a purpose or to make some type of impression on the world, no matter how small or whether we ever know what it is or not. Originally we were created sinless, in the likeness or image of God to reflect his glory to all creation, and yet we chose to sin, to corrupt that image, and now we are in dire straits, and without a Savior we are without hope. Now most of you reading this have made a profession of faith in Jesus, and have escaped the wrath of God against sin. You know that eternity awaits all men, and it is just a matter of where they will spend eternity; either in the presence of God (heaven), or enduring the wrath of God for eternity in hell. But if we are saved, what kind of impression should we be making on an unsaved world, especially one that now seems to be spiraling hopelessly out of control?

Now what in the world does all this have to do with the current pandemic or the vitriol of expressions heard on the necessity or non-essentiality of taking the current vaccine for this Covid outbreak? Now to be honest, I do not know what kind of propaganda is going on in the rest of the world, but if it is anything like it is here in the U.S. it seems to be reaching, shall we say, pandemic levels. And who are we to believe? Now lest you get me wrong, there is a real pandemic going on and people are dying, and it appears to most that the vaccine is doing some good. Maybe not to extent that some had hoped, yet I will leave you to your own personnel experts that you listen to as to its effectiveness.

We have all heard the rhetoric on each side of the issue of whether or not to vaccinate. Those who demand mandatory or forced vaccinations say that those who refuse are being selfish and putting others in harm's way, and are a detriment to the well-being of society; maybe they are right. The other side say they have the right to do with their body as they choose, the vaccine isn't yet proven, and for many I think it is that they don't like anyone telling them what to do; "you aren't the boss of me."

But if we could delve down deep into the psyche of this whole mess, I think we might find that people are simply scared of dying. There is a great fear of that great unknown, not so much because it can't be known, but because it is known. Maybe not on the conscious level, but everyone knows that someday, somehow, they must stand before God and give an account for what they have done in the body. For the Christian, there should be no fear in dying; apprehension perhaps, but not fear. Our concern should be in proclaiming the gospel to all of those within our sphere who are afraid and have no hope.

God is sovereign, and the fact of the matter is that unless Jesus returns first, you and I are going to die in some manner, and the day of that death has already been pre-determined. Vaccine or not, I cannot add one day to the life God has determined that I live. Perhaps my decision not to get the vaccine is His means of taking me out of this world by allowing me to get sick from this covid and die. But it could also be His means of showing to others that He is sovereign as to who will or will not get sick from this virus. At a certain point we all have to make a decision (and who knows we may change our mind), and trust that God knows what He is doing. For me personally it is not yet the time to get a vaccine.

I wasn't going to go into this, but I was asked yesterday, and I fear they misunderstood what I was trying to convey, so I will somewhat explain it now, realizing that for an e-mail it is getting excessive. They thought I meant that I was trusting in God that I wouldn't catch the virus, and so I didn't need the vaccine. I am saying that I am trusting Christ (God) with my soul, and I am trusting God with my life. If He so desires (and I hope He doesn't) that I get covid, so be it. But I had much rather leave my life in His hands, than in governments and institutions that SAY they have my best interest in mind. Until that time comes when they can once again say with sincerity of heart "In God we Trust" and prove it by their actions, it is hard to trust a government which constantly seems to do its utmost to legitimize the most heinous of sinful behavior, and at the same time try to convince me of its morality.

Now I have rambled on quite long enough, and reading over what I have written, I realize I have only scratched the surface, and perhaps have muddied the waters instead of clarifying it. But I want to leave you with just one last instance before closing, and ponder this carefully. You are all familiar with the story of Shadrach, Meshach, and Abednego, in the book of Daniel. It is in chapter 3, and to make it short, they were to bow down and worship an image or lose their lives in fire. Now I would really like to go off here on another topic, but we need to end. They refused to compromise their belief in the one God, even to the point of death, and listen to what their reply was. Oh that every Christian, would have this heart, "Our God whom we serve is able to deliver us from the burning fiery furnace, and he will deliver us out of your hand, O king. (And here is the important part) But if not, be it known to you O king that we will not serve your gods....."

God can and is able to preserve us from all harm, BUT IF NOT, if it is God's will that we perish under the ravages of this virus so be it. But to place my life in the hands of a government INSTEAD of in the hands of God, is not something I can do at this time. "I will lift up my eyes to the hills- from whence comes my help? My help comes from the Lord who made heaven and earth."

Where does your help come from? Until next time, Shalom.

PSALM 25:4-5

There were two topics on my mind this morning, this passage in psalms and a couple of sermons I read dealing with past epidemics. They were much more severe then what we have going on today, but it was a less traveled time, and so while there were many deaths, it didn't turn into a pandemic. And while some of what I read was very applicable to today, I am like most of you, tired of everything I hear or see being about politics or the virus, or the mixture of the two. In the midst of all this turmoil and misinformation (on all sides I am afraid) it is good for the Christian to lift up his soul to heaven and to sing with the psalmist, "You are the God of my salvation, on you I wait all the day long."

However, it is the first part of verses 4-5 that we will concentrate on. "Make me know your ways O Jehovah; teach me your paths; make me walk in your truth and teach me." Then it ends with what we looked at before, "For you are the God of my salvation; on you I wait all the day long."

How many of you pray that or something similar on a regular basis? Perhaps you think everything you need to know on your pilgrimage will just pop automatically into your head. But this is much more than that. It is an active participation on our part, but at the same time calling upon God to make us learn. The Hebrew word to teach here is lamad and has a primitive root of to goad. As oxen were often goaded to go in the correct direction, so the student needs to be led or guided in the correct direction.

Is it the desire of your heart to know the ways of God, and that He would guide you to walk in those truths? If He is the God of your salvation, then He is also your Shepard, and He will not allow one of his sheep to stray very far, and if need be, He will use the rod of correction to guide you on the right path.

The start of this psalm begins with the psalmist crying out "To You O LORD I lift up my soul," and those who can join him in this chorus will also join him in asking that God would work on their behalf. That He would make us know His ways and paths in order that we might walk in truth. It is the desire of our heart because He is the God of our salvation, and we find our pleasure in those ways which glorify Him.

Do you find your greatest pleasure in knowing God and glorifying Him? Do you wait all the day long for Him and as another psalm says as the deer pants for water, so my soul pants for God? Does your soul thirst for God? I am afraid most of us spend very little time in this state of mind, yet it should attend our every thought, for He is the God of our Salvation.

Think on these things, and until next time, May the Lord bless you and keep you; May His face shine upon you and be gracious to you; May the Lord lift up His countenance upon you and give you peace. Shalom.

NO OTHER NAME

"And there is salvation in no one else, for there is no other name under heaven given among men by which they must be saved."- Acts 4:12 (ESV)

"See to it that no one takes you captive by philosophy and empty deceit, according to human tradition, according to elemental spirits of the world, and not according to Christ."-Colossians 2:8 (ESV)

"Guard what was committed to your trust, avoiding the profane and vain babblings and contradictions of what is falsely called knowledge-by professing it some have strayed concerning the faith."-1 Timothy 6:20-21

Sitting above my desk are four books which I consider as the most influential which the world has ever known. Karl Marx's Das Kapital along with the Communist Manifesto, Charles Darwin's Origin of Species, The Quran (Koran), and of course the Bible. Three written by men, and one by God, penned by man. There are of course many other influential books in existence, some no doubt that inspired these men, but it is the result of their work that is most known. I keep them there as a reminder that ideas have consequences, even if it is many years later. Now it is not my intention to give a history lesson, or an in depth look at these books, but to help remind ourselves where much of the insanity we see going on all around us came from. Most, if not all of the ideologies we see currently swirling around us, are nothing more than a power grab, a power grab for the souls of men. Pick one and follow it to its roots and see if evolution and some type of economic communalism is not at its roots. And both of these are, when boiled down to their essence, simply a means in which one group of men justifies itself in enslaving another.

Now in some ways I would like nothing more than to spend a great deal of time explaining this further. But that isn't really the gist of what I wanted to write about, just an introduction into what affects us even more as Christians, and that is a Christianity that has allowed itself to become compromised by worldly philosophies. As one writer has put it, can it really be Christianity if it holds to some of those views the world espouses? By that we mean those views that go directly against scriptural teachings. How did we get here, and in my little realm of the world these things seem so far away, so why should I be concerned about them? These are not illegitimate questions, and as a Christian disciple it may be you have much more pressing issues than what is the latest philosophical fad.

Now each week as many as ten or fifteen topics might perk my interest on what to write about, and usually it is the last one that gets chosen. This doesn't mean it is the most important or interesting, but it usually is the one chosen, and this week is no exception. I had intended on spending two or three weeks going over John Calvin's work on the "Life of a Christian man", and probably (?) will get to it next time, but felt compelled to write a brief note on an article I had just finished reading.

Many of you are familiar with B.B. Warfield, and he wrote an article called "Christless Christianity" which you can find in the Harvard Theological Review of 1912 pp. 423-473, or in his collected works, vol.3. As you can see, this was written over a hundred years ago, but in it he deals with several of the idealisms or criticisms of the current day in which he lived, and of which we have reaped the results. Much of it had to do with the higher criticisms of that era, most specifically dealing with the historic Jesus. It is interesting to note as you are probably already aware of, that in many instances there is a significant difference when they speak of the historic Jesus and the historic Christ. Now I must admit that he (Warfield) must have been a most mature Christian not to completely go unhinged over some of the things these men were saying. Let me give you a couple of them and see if it is not as disturbing to you as it was to me.

"Though Jesus should be proved never to have existed, the truth which has come down to us...the establishment of holy relations with our Heavenly Father would still be true...a historical Jesus is unnecessary."-Frank H. Foster

"My inmost religious convictions would suffer no harm, even if I now felt obliged to conclude that Jesus never lived"- "Jesus in Modern Criticism" E.T. 1907 p.85

There are other similar quotes sprinkled throughout this article and throughout Warfield shows the futility of their thinking, but despite all this, we deal with some of the same attitudes today. But this just demonstrates what happens when humanistic philosophy infiltrates the church. And so a brief, very brief history of the Age of Enlightenment when human reason seemed to gain the upper hand, and how its fruit can be seen today. Begun in the 1700's, we see how by the middle of the 1800's religious thought had begun to be corrupted by rationalism. Of course we know that the gospel is always foolish to those who have not been spiritually awakened as we see in Corinthians, but now it seemed as if the enemies of Christ had a new weapon to wield. But we see also that this newly found humanism, which is really as old as the Garden of Eden, led to two world wars, mass extinctions, and the reintroduction of communism. If you don't know what I mean by the reintroduction of communism, ask sometime and I will explain my thoughts on it. But also this Christless Christianity led to the moral and social failures of the 1960's. These weren't behaviors that didn't already exist, but it was an openness that these behaviors were no longer wrong, and they began to become socially acceptable. Now here we are 60 years later and we are seeing the fruits and expansions of these types of attitudes. I could be wrong, but it would not surprise me if Sodom and Gomorrah are not blushing at some of the things they see us commit.

But to get back to the individual who calls him or herself a Christian, what does all this have to do with me? We spend a lot of time looking back at events that affected our lives, but we don't spend much time thinking upon the ramifications of those events. But these ideologies and events have led us to where we are today. Social justice, black lives matter, the latest fad of critical race theory, political correctness, and a host of other things are seemingly crowding out our Christianity. How do we cope with such things? I want to end today with three questions that every Christian should ask themselves, and as I wrote this I decided four questions. Unless I forget, it would be good to answer this next time, for when we have solid answers for these questions, I believe we will not find it necessary to get quite so anxious over the current pandemic of ideology, which seems to be worse than the pandemic of covid-19.

So, if you are a Christian, WHO are you? How is it or WHAT has happened that you can go about proclaiming to be a Christian? Thirdly, HOW was this accomplished? We will answer this next time, but we can't help from saying that if you think it was something you did, than it will just as easily be something you could undo. And lastly, and it is hard to refrain from answering now, but WHY are you a Christian? And as we close, I want to remind you of our first verse, and one which should always be on our mind.

"And there is salvation in no one else, (Jesus) for there is no other name under heaven given among men by which they must be saved."- Acts 4:12

Shalom my friends, and until next time may the Lord bless you and keep you, and may his face shine upon you.

TO THE PRAISE OF THE GLORY OF HIS GRACE

"To the praise of the glory of His grace."-Ephesians 1:6

Last week we sort of ended by asking how Christians can allow themselves to get caught up or deceived by some of the prevailing philosophies of the day. These are not new philosophies of course, just old ones rehashed, but rationalism has so crept into society and by extension the church, that Christianity no longer has a standard definition. Interestingly, the dictionary definition begins by stating that Christianity is the religion derived from Jesus Christ, based on the bible as sacred scripture. On the surface this is correct, but personally I find it shallow and deceptive because it is incomplete. Again, what is the definition of religion? Religion is "a personal set or institutionalized system of religious attitudes, beliefs, and practices." So we can say using these definitions, that Islam is the religion derived from Mohammed, based on the Quran as sacred scripture. Do you see now why I find this definition of Christianity insulting? It equates it on an equal footing with any other set of beliefs out there, which is simply false. But the number of professing Christians out there who do not see the difference, is staggering, and so we asked or stated, that it is vital that the Christian disciple know who they are. So do you know who or what you are, do you know what a Christian is?

Now some of you who receive this e-mail heard a sermon yesterday which actually contained part of what I wanted to say, and I wish I had of sent this out last week, because now it would seem as if I were following on the coattails of someone else. That happens sometimes when you try to limit the size of an e-mail, so we will skip over most of it, and just say that as a Christian, you have been adopted into God's family, and you are now no longer a citizen of this world, but a citizen of the kingdom of God on pilgrimage through the rest of your time of life on this earth. (See Hebrews 11:13)

There is more, but what happened that you can now call yourself a member of God's family and His kingdom? This is what differentiates Christianity from religion, or if you prefer, other religions, in that it is God who chose you or adopted you and made you a citizen of His kingdom. Anyone can wake up one morning and decide to become a Muslim, or Buddhist or Hindu, or whatever, the only requirements being to follow those particular teachings, but one cannot become a Christian by simply adhering to a bunch of rules or doctrine; you must be born again (regenerated or made new). Unfortunately there are many within the Christian community who teach and practice decisional regeneration, but it is an unbiblical practice. Jesus speaks on this in John chapter three and in other places, but you must be born again of the Spirit. You are regenerated by the Holy Spirit and then have saving faith in Christ, not the other way around. It is not our intention here to spend a great deal of time on this one aspect, on proofs, etc., but simply to reiterate that the only reason you are a Christian, is because God chose you.

So these attitudes, beliefs and practices you have are not because they belong to some institutionalized system, but because these attitudes and beliefs and practices are who you are, albeit imperfectly lived out in this life. What I am trying to get at is that there are many who profess to be Christian and live the Christian life, but do not believe in the inerrancy of scripture or the atonement, or in some cases (as we saw previously) in the necessity of it all, without which, how can they call themselves Christian? This is why it is so necessary to know who you are, what happened, and next, how it was accomplished.

I know it should seem really basic and elementary, but there really are some people out there who adhere to a Christless Christianity, and don't realize the absurdity of that statement. Without Jesus, the Christ, there is no Christianity and there is no salvation. Like I said, this is stuff that any second grader could understand, but as Jude said, certain men have crept in unaware and deny the only Lord God and our Lord Jesus Christ. And they use philosophies and higher criticisms and so called education to try and deceive the very elect, and confuse those who are weak in the faith.

But our salvation was accomplished by the death of Christ, and our righteousness was accomplished by the life of Christ, and these were imputed to us. God's justice demands that the penalty of sin (death) must be met. Righteousness demands that justice be done; otherwise God is not God, and who besides Jesus has lived a sinless life that could be imputed to our behalf? Now I realize nearly everyone I am writing to knows this, but not necessarily everyone, and besides, it is good to remind ourselves on a regular basis who we are, what happened, and how it was accomplished that we can call ourselves Christian.

A true Christian will at times struggle with one issue or another, and because there are many things that are spiritually discerned, we may not have the answers that those who are antagonistic may ask. Or, we may have the answer, but it is not the one they want to hear, so they dismiss it as error. In one way or another, Satan has been asking these types of questions from the very beginning, so we shouldn't be too surprised if those under his sway do the same. And such were some of us at one time, questioning those who all along were trying to tell us the true way to life, and now we know; Jesus is the way the truth and the life, and no one comes to the Father but by Him. And do you ever wonder why unregenerate people ask these questions? Now it could be God is working on their hearts, but usually it is because it is the only way they can manifest their hatred towards God. In a sense I would like to go off on a rabbit trail here, because it is important to know. Antagonism against us is not necessarily because they hate us, but because they hate God, and so take it out on us, because we are the people of God. And so we see how Stephen in the book of Acts, can say "Lord do not charge them with this sin"; not that they weren't guilty, but because they did not know what they are doing.

We have perhaps strayed a little, but the Christian disciple knows who they are, what has happened to make them who they are, and how it was accomplished. This doesn't mean everyone knows all the little details: isn't the gist of it, believe in the Lord Jesus Christ and you will be saved? Whosoever shall believe in Him shall not perish but have eternal life? Or, (Acts 2:38) "Repent and let ever one of you be baptized in the name of Jesus Christ for the remission of sins; and you will receive the gift of the Holy Spirit." Sometimes we want to make it so complicated, (and there are things hard to understand) but there is much to be said for having a child like faith. But at the end of it all, why has God done all of this? Why has He allowed the suffering and death of His only begotten Son? What is man that He is mindful of him? Why has He reconciled to Himself those who were at enmity with Him? It is to or for the praise of the glory of His grace.

This is the Christian life; to praise His glorious grace. How often do you meditate on this truth? I really want to go further here, but it would be a distraction. Do you comprehend this; to the praise of the glory of His grace? I will speak no further except to ask you to dwell upon this intently for the next few days, (though we will do so throughout eternity) and until next time, Shalom.

WATERMELON AND MANNA

In just a few days we will be celebrating the thanksgiving holiday, a tradition we have had here in America for many years. But are we really celebrating it (if that is even a correct way of describing it) in the way that it was meant, a day of thanksgiving to God for His provision throughout the year? I would say that most Christians will give thanks of some sort, but how many will just say a perfunctory prayer and then go about the festivities of the day? Maybe I am wrong about this, but sometimes giving lip service is worse than saying nothing at all; where is your heart at? But lest we get too sidetracked, remember what God has provided and be thankful.

Most of us are familiar with the details of how God brought the Jewish people out of the land of Egypt where they had been slaves for many years. They were free and no longer in bondage, but it wasn't long before they were complaining about what they were going to eat, so God provided them with the bread from heaven, Manna, and the only thing they had to do was go gather it. But, they were only to gather what they needed for the day, and they found out quickly that it turned rotten the next day if they gathered too much. Except for the sixth day, in which they were to gather enough for two days, so they could rest on the Sabbath. And you can read it for yourself, that God was angry with those who went out to gather on the Sabbath, though there was nothing to gather.

But as many of us are prone to do, they soon grew tired of God's provisions, and desired more. Some of them begin to grumble and wished they were still slaves in Egypt, so they could have their watermelon, onions, leeks, etc. Now we read that it was the mixed multitude that had come out with the Israelites that instigated the complaining, and as is usually the case, they drew many into their way of complaint.

Now by way of analogy, and to keep this short, let us compare a few things and see if it doesn't very well relate to us as well. When we become Christians, we are set free from the bondage of sin, and become God's people. He has taken on the responsibility of providing for our needs, and all we have to do is go gather it. And usually, though not in each case, He provides much more than what we need, but how many of us are satisfied with it? We talk much about contentedness, and well we should, but how many of us out there are saying "I need just a little bit more." After all I need a new truck to haul around this travel trailer you have given me, and once we get to that camping spot we will need a four wheeler to get around. Don't forget about a satellite system to watch our sports and television programs, after all, what are we going to do when it gets dark outside. Of course I am exaggerating this a little bit (?) but this is how we tend to think.

What I really want us to think about though, is not the material side of things so much, as it is the spiritual. We have been set free from slavery to the ways of this world, and now are slaves of righteousness; we are to do those things that are right. It should be our pleasure to do what is right, for that is one of the reasons we have been recreated for. We have been set free from sin, and not only that, but many of the legitimate activities we participated in are no longer to vie for our time. Maybe this is a little out of context, but when Paul said that when he was a child he spoke, thought and acted like a child, but when he became a man, he put away childish things, it was for our edification. At a certain point we need to realize we are to put away childish things; if the shoe fits wear it.

It has been said by more than one person, and I think we could all attest to the fact that life wasn't that difficult until we became a Christian. We just did what we wanted to do, and it was okay. As long as everyone else is doing it, and it isn't against the law, (which in this day and time rioting and looting seem to be okay) and if you can protest and say it is your right, than anything goes. If the world system says it is okay, it's okay. But now, we realize that it isn't okay to participate in much of what the world does, because God says that is not the right way to live. And if we are not careful and attentive, we will allow the mixed multitude, those who are not Christian, but with whom we come into contact with, to influence our attitude. We may, though we shouldn't, begin to say to ourselves that life was better under slavery. Then I could do this, and then I could do that, and let's face it, many times sin is pleasurable. But it is fleeting.

There is a passage which always encourages me whenever sin rears its ugly head or when those legitimate activities seem to be causing an inordinate amount of time or thought to be spent on them. It is the great faith passage we find in Hebrews 11, especially when it speaks of Moses.

"By faith Moses, when he became of age, refused to be called the son of Pharaoh's daughter, choosing rather to suffer affliction with the people of God than to enjoy the passing pleasures of sin, esteeming the reproach of Christ greater riches than the treasure in Egypt; for he looked to the reward."-Hebrews 11:24-26.

Most of us will never have access to the riches that Moses had available to him, nor to that mass availability of sinful pleasures that he had on account of being the adopted son of Pharaoh's daughter. And by these passing or fleeting pleasures it could very well mean a lifetime. But what will it profit a man if he gains the whole world and yet loses his soul? Even Solomon in his old age declares to us the vanity of this life being spent in the pursuit of wealth and pleasure. But as it is really God the Holy Spirit speaking to us, shouldn't we pay a little more attention to what is being said?

So as we come to our thanksgiving dinners and activities this week, let us be a little more mindful and thankful for the seemingly drudgeries of this life, and be grateful for the manna that God has provided over the last year. It won't be that long before we are in the Promised Land, and then we can truly feast.

Think on these things, and hopefully they will bless you, and until the next time, may the peace of God be with you. Shalom.

TO EVERYONE TO WHOM MUCH IS GIVEN

I think all Christians would agree that all scripture is given by inspiration of God and is inerrant (to not think so should call into question your boldness in calling yourself by that name) and it is authoritative over our lives. So whenever we read our bibles, it should be as if God is speaking to us directly, and informing us of what we need to know on various things. But, whenever we read those words which Jesus spoke during his time here on earth, it seems like we are getting a double dose; God in the flesh speaking to us, and maybe we should pay even more attention to what is being revealed to us.

Now in the passage in Luke that our verse is going to come from, Jesus is speaking to a large crowd and to his disciples about the value of laying up treasure in heaven, and wise stewardship, and the cost of discipleship. Then in Luke 12:48, we read those words of Jesus which tells us, "For everyone to whom much is given, from him much will be required; and to whom much has been committed, of him they will ask the more." This isn't unusual, for if you are an employer you expect more from those who you give more responsibility to, or pay more but it also works that way in the Kingdom of God. But we shouldn't just look at it as a simple statement that Jesus uses to clarify what he has been teaching, but also consider it as a command. We could look at the parable of the talents in Matthew 25 and see that God expects us to use the gifts and abilities he has given us in a profitable manner. This entails many things that we don't have time to fully discuss, but we could easily make the argument that it is primarily for the edification of others. Our daily needs are for the most part easily obtained, so what is the excess being used for?

Everyone realizes that different people receive different gifts, and to varying degrees, but it is all to be used for the edification of others. If it is the gift of ministry, then minister, if it is in encouraging others, then encourage, if in teaching, then teach, and we could go on. But if you only minister to yourself, or encourage yourself, or teach yourself, isn't that gift going to waste? It is as if you were hiding your talent in the ground, and we know what became of that individual in the parable. Now you may be saying that to whom much is given, much is required, but I haven't received much, so I am not responsible. Do you really think that is going to fly with God? You already know the answer, but you somehow think it doesn't apply to you. But, it applies to each and every one of us.

There is coming a day when each of us will stand before the judgement seat of God to receive the rewards of what was done in the body here on earth. Some, who have never placed their faith in the finished work of Christ, will receive the reward of eternal damnation. We who have placed our faith in Christ will receive the reward of eternal life, but not only that, we will receive rewards for a job well done. Dwelling for eternity in the presence of God, communing face to face with our Savior Jesus would be reward enough, but there is even more. 1 Corinthians 2:9 is a verse which we should all have memorized, and it is an incredible, cross that out, it is a majestic truth that surpasses all understanding. "It is written that eye hath not seen, nor ear heard, neither have entered into the heart of man, the things which God hath prepared for those who love Him." What an incredible reward is that?

So where are you storing up your treasures or rewards? Are you using the talents that God has given you to gather up earthly treasure that either perishes with the using, or where moth and thief destroy it? God allows us to have earthly pleasures, but are you using it solely for your own pleasure and lusts? How many Christians have an overabundance, yet never tithe? I think we are beginning to stray, but how much have you been given? As to what it is and how much, only you and God know, but are you using it to his glory? God is glorified in many ways, but we bring dishonor, disgrace and indignity to His honor, grace, and dignity when we do not use those gifts which he has given us to make his glory known.

How are you doing in this area or arena (for we are being watched by multitudes of beings, some physical, and some spiritual) in using your gifts to glorify God? I cannot speak for you, but sometimes when I write these things, I realize how negligent I am in proclaiming the greatness of our God and Savior Jesus Christ; isn't that what we are about? To whom much is given, much is required. We are to use our gifts in such a way as to not only glorify God, but to edify our neighbor, especially our fellow brothers and sisters in Christ, and to make our light so shine before all men that they may see our good works, and glorify our God in heaven. Are you doing that to the best of the abilities that God has given you? Think on this, and hopefully this has been useful to you. Until we meet again, may the Lord bless you and keep you and may his face shine upon you. Shalom.

RESOLUTIONS AGAIN?

Over the past several years it has been my habit to write something on New Year's resolutions, and this year will be no exception. Not because we can't make resolutions at any other time of the year, but it is a time we think of new beginnings. We resolved to do something the previous year, but life got in the way and we didn't do what we had resolved to do. But, it was important to us, so we want to give it another shot. Christians are no exception, and while it is good to be examining ourselves on a regular basis, (not just once a year) the beginning of a New Year is a good time to sit and reflect where you have been and where you are going. Are you walking worthy of the Name by which you have been called, or have the distractions of life choked out the word, and blocked your path? Now is a good time to weed out those thorns of distraction.

It is perhaps also wise to consider those hindrances in your pathway, and see if they are not cherished idols. Idols which have such a strong hold on your life, that you are unwilling to let them go, and if that is the case, is Christ really your Savior, or just, as they used to say, a balm to ease your wicked soul. Matthew Mead wrote a short book entitled "The Almost Christian Discovered", and it would do some good to read it if you get the chance. It would be good to give a lot of quotes from the book, but we would do well to remember what he says, in that many a time it is just one lust which keeps us from Christ. Not that we don't profess Christ, but we don't possess Christ. We are almost Christian, but not quite. We become hindered by that one sin we refuse to give up, and sooner or later it will cause us to part from our profession, and reveal who we really are; sons destined to destruction.

But again, now is a good time to see if those old sins which were done away with, have not crept back into your life. Not that you cherish them as a false professor would, but you haven't been as diligent in your warfare as you could be. As we examine our life, we might see many areas, or maybe just specific areas we need to work or grow in, so we repent and confess our sin and shortcomings, and resolve to do better. This is something that needs to be done on a regular basis, perhaps even daily, but the Christian desires to do better and become more Christ like, and resolves to do so.

Most of you know I have a high regard for the works of Jonathan Edwards, and each year I encourage you to read through the seventy resolutions he had for his own life. Some of them seem similar to one another, but for the most part they are different. It would be good to concentrate on one of these each year, but we may not make it that long. So we will look at two of them very briefly, and see if they may not be good examples for each of us to follow in our own life. Number 43 is "Resolved. Never, henceforward, till I die, to act as if I were any way my own, but entirely and altogether God's." Number 48, "Resolved, Constantly, with the utmost niceness and diligence, and the strictest scrutiny, to be looking into the state of my soul, that I may know whether I have truly an interest in Christ or not; that when I come to die, I may not have any negligence respecting this to repent of."

You can easily see how these two are related, for the man or individual who knows they are in Christ, having been born again, and adopted by God, instinctively knows that he is not his own, but belongs to Christ. His life will not be one of harboring the least of sin, but a lifelong struggle against all known sin. Though there may be many battles lost, yet he wars against those activities and attitudes which hinder his Christian walk. The Christian life is not one of walking an aisle, making a profession of faith, and then ignoring it all as if it was just another day in the life; it is life and meant to be lived. There is more to say on this subject, but back to resolutions.

Now is a really good time of the year to think on these things, for it is a time when we think of new beginnings. It is a time to refocus on what you may have allowed to be neglected, whatever that might be. Has your prayer time been neglected to the point of seldom speaking with God, or perhaps you have let your reading of scripture dwindle to no more than once a week when your pastor has you open your bible? If so, then your walk as a Christian has no more effectiveness in the world, then the non-Christian, for your attention is on the things of this life, and not the things of eternity. Search yourself, and see if this is not the case, or you might even know someone else whose faith SEEMS ineffective. We must be careful when judging others, and it would do much more good to judge ourselves, and concentrate on our own deficiencies.

We can search the scriptures and know the will of God, and what He resolves for our life, but we make resolutions in order to remind us that His will is what is important, not ours. It is a reminder to do better. But we cannot do better on our own, but must depend upon God even in this area. Jonathan Edwards had this little note at the beginning of his resolutions, which we must not forget.

"Being sensible that I am unable to do anything without God's help, I do humbly entreat Him, by his grace, to enable me to keep these resolutions, so far as they are agreeable to his will, for Christ's sake."

It is good to make resolutions, but only if you are serious about them. We are speaking here of Christian duties, not those of losing weight, getting exercise, etc., though they should be serious also, but those duties that we should be doing anyway. But resolutions make us concentrate on those areas that may have been neglected, or in which we need to grow. But they should be godly resolutions, and as such, it will only be successful if we rely on God for help. It is also helpful to write them down and look at them on a regular basis. Daily is probably best, but don't be like me and put it in your wallet and forget about it. Just as an aside, I got a new wallet for Christmas, and I found a couple of resolutions I had written for myself over ten years ago, and had forgotten it was in there. It does no good if you forget your own resolution, but perhaps we might talk more about this aspect next time.

As we start a new year, let us renew our efforts to walk more Christ like, loving our neighbors as ourselves and God with our whole being. Let us not be quite so concerned about the trivial things of everyday life, such as stock markets and government elections and scandals and media madness, but let us concentrate on the souls of men and eternity. In the end, this is what matters, so in that respect, let us set our affection on things above, for our life as it concerns worldly things is over. And also to this end, we must proclaim the gospel to all creatures for eternity is at stake. If we would just resolve to remember that there is an eternity, much of this would fall into place.

Think on these things, and until next time, Shalom.

A RETURN TO MORTIFICATION AND REPENTANCE

About a month ago we wrote a short post on mortification and its necessity for growth in the Christian life. We are going to add a few more thoughts towards that in this post, always keeping in mind that without the help of the Holy Spirit, most of our strivings will be in vain. However this does not give us an excuse to be negligent in our duty or to use it as an excuse when we fail to completely kill off those sins which so easily beset us. But it seems like most of us, or at least in my own case, that we fail in the same area over and over again, and it begs the question; do we take our salvation seriously? All of us would answer in the affirmative, so what seems to be the problem?

I truly believe the answers are not that difficult. The difficulty lies in putting these answers into practice. Now it could be that some or most of you do not struggle with any issues in the Christian life, and I hope that is true, but for the rest of us the question WHY keeps popping up. Why do I continue to struggle in this same area, when I know it is wrong or God has made it clear it is not something He approves of for your life? By that I mean God has told you not to participate in some activity, though for others participation may not be wrong. There is nothing wrong per se with playing golf, but if God has called you to spend your time in more worthwhile pursuits, then playing golf is wrong for you. Not only is it wrong, but if you know He has forbidden you to do so, then it is sin. It is these kinds of things which cause us anguish. In our desire to keep one foot in the world, and one foot in heaven, we compromise our principles.

But our ethical principles, morality and spirituality are so connected and intertwined, that we forget that it is possible to be ethical and moral, but at the same time deny our spirituality, or our Christianity. Using the example above, there is nothing unethical or immoral about playing golf, but if God has told you no, then there is a sense in which you deny your spiritual relationship to God, if you play. Again, if you have not had to deal with this issue it is somewhat harder to understand, but for those of us who do go through these situations, it can at times be quite dramatic.

This could be a long post, for we are just touching on some of those areas in "The Obedience of Faith", but I want to give a few quotes from C.B. Eavey from his book on the Principles of Christian Ethics. Hopefully these will stir up your mind and will be an exhortation to keep running the race that is set before us. We are told to keep our eyes on Christ, the author and finisher of our faith, and if we properly understood those words we wouldn't have near the problems we do. But sometimes we need to hear exhortation in different words, so here are some quotes by Mr. Eavey.

"Whatever our professions, we do not live on a very high level of spirituality when we are lax in moral life."

"He who would live righteously must contend against foes within and enemies without."

"When we Christians make compromise with sin, when we violate moral principles, when we are careless or negligent in living, when we quench the Spirit in His promptings to duty, we bring blight upon our spirituality, dim our vision of God, weaken our moral character, discredit the Gospel, and dishonor the holy name of Him whose we profess to be. Moral living is not a pleasant kind of daydreaming."

How easy it is to drift back into a lifestyle of not necessarily sin, but a stupor concerning the Christian life. When we don't completely kill those sins in our life which so easily beset or snare us, they will eventually regain life and cause us trouble again. And why is it we don't completely kill it? Is there something deep down within us that thinks that God might change His mind and allow us to return to those old ways? Or maybe we think that if we do enough good works that God will look the other way if we reward ourselves with some sin. Maybe we could come up with a hundred other reasons, but the fact of the matter is we need to repent.

We are talking about Christians not unbelievers, and we wonder how we could have strayed so far. It is because we have quit listening to God, whether in His word or in the preaching of the word. We hear it with our ears and read it on the pages of the bible, but we are not listening to the Holy Spirit as He instructs us.

"Cease listening to instruction my son, and you will stray from the words of knowledge"-Proverbs 19:27

For whatever reason, whether pride or indifference or some other type of sin, you have decided to quit listening or taking seriously the Holy Spirit's teaching. We need to repent and return to our first love of Jesus Christ. Go and read those first few chapters in the book of Revelation and see what Jesus said to those seven churches. Then examine your own life and see if the message to those churches could be said to you individually as well. If so, do as most of them were to do, and that is to repent. When we stray or wander off from the words of knowledge, it doesn't happen overnight. It is a gradual thing and for the most part it happens so slowly that you will never notice it.

But God will get your attention one way or another. He doesn't exactly use these words, but He lets us know that we can do this the easy way or the hard way. As Christians, we are His adopted children, and if we need discipline He will provide it. We have so many different types of exhortations in scripture not to be disobedient, but one of my favorites is not to be a stubborn ass. I sometimes think it is my favorite because it fits so well.

Repenting of our sin and admitting once again that our hearts have grown cold to the ways of God is not always easy. How often do we look in the mirror and see the exact type of person we see in Isaiah 58? A person who seeks God daily and delights to know His ways and yet at the same time is full of sin and transgressions. Or have we gone so far that God speaks to you as He does in Psalm 50 and ask you personally, "What right have you to declare My statutes, or take My covenant in your mouth, seeing you hate instruction and cast My words behind you?" God is speaking to the wicked, and in verse 22 continues: "Now consider this, you who forget God, lest I tear you in pieces."

"Now consider this", could be speaking to those who are wicked, but it could very well be speaking to those who are really His people and have strayed from the paths of righteousness. In either case, it is a call to repentance. God, throughout the bible has been telling sinful man to turn from their evil ways. As we read in Acts17, there was a time when God overlooked the ignorance of man, but now He commands all men everywhere to repent; there is coming a day of judgement.

Since we are primarily writing this to those who are already Christians, what is it you need to repent about? If you are like me, it could be a number of things, not just one, but if you aren't sure, just ask God and He will guide you. At the end of Psalm 139 we read these words, "Search me O God, and know my heart; try me, and know my anxieties; and see if there is any wicked way in me, and lead me in the way everlasting." God already knows these things, but this is a prayer for God to show them to our face in order that we can repent. When was the last time you truly got before the throne of God and repented of your sin?

Think on these things, and until we meet next, Shalom.

1 TIMOTHY 6

As the reader can tell, we are getting very near the end of this book. Except for the chapter "Point of no return", these last four chapters were never posted on the website, blog, or FB. In a sense they are much more personal to me, but seeing how it might be useful to others, they are being included.

So how do we explain God's dealing with us, without airing our dirty laundry? Not that it is any dirtier than the next person's, but for the most part people are interested in gossip. Instead of focusing on what we might be able to learn from one another's mistakes, we are comparing ourselves to others, judging whether or not we are better than them. There is a sense in which we are accountable to one another, but ultimately it is to Jesus that we are accountable. When we stand before His throne one day, He isn't going to ask how we did compared to Joe down the street, but will judge us according to righteousness, and it is only His righteousness imputed to us that is going to matter. God does not grade on the curve. With that being said, if anyone wants to know specifics, then just ask. If I don't know you or don't trust you, then what is written here is sufficient.

Are you covetous, desiring what belongs to others? Or maybe you are just greedy, wanting more and more? Now there are a lot of exceptions out there, but if we are honest, most of us just want more then we have. There is a lack of satisfaction in what God has given us. Whatever that might be, God has provided jobs for all of us, and it could be that you are the janitor this year and five years from now you are the CEO of that same company. Or it could be that 25 years from now you are still the janitor and have seen many others climb what we might call the ladder of success.

We are specifically dealing with Christians in this article, so as a Christian, are you satisfied or contented with being that janitor for 25 years? Let's assume that you are being paid enough to live off of, but if you have a family, is it still enough? Does your spouse have to work or do you have to take on a part time job in order to pay the bills? This is the situation of more people then we might think, and in a lot, if not in most cases, it is because of debt. This is a whole other issue that we are not going to be looking at today, but how did our indebtedness occur? There are some very legitimate reasons for incurring debt, but isn't it for the most part just a result of us not being content with what God has given us?

As we go through parts of 1 Timothy 6, each one of us needs to examine ourselves and ask, am I living this way? This is written directly to you Christian, God expects us to take it to heart. If you are like me, you already know these things, but knowing them and living them aren't quite the same are they?

"But godliness with contentment is great gain, for we brought nothing into this world, and we cannot take anything out of this world. But if we have food and clothing, with these we will be content."-1 Tim. 6:6-7 (ESV)

This is very reminiscent of what Job says after he had lost all his possessions. "Naked I came from my mother's womb, and naked shall I return. The Lord gave, and the Lord has taken away; blessed be the name of the LORD." These can only be the words of a man who is content with what God has given him. Don't get me wrong, there isn't necessarily anything wrong with wanting more, but are we content with what we have?

So getting back to making this more personal, about 4years ago, after having been out of the workforce for a couple of years, I decided to start selling more stuff online. I was already selling some, but decided buying storage lockers would greatly increase the amount of items I would have available for sell. Now if you remember from the introduction, all I really want to do is teach theology and the bible in some venue. I really don't have any other ambition, and if I am not doing that, then I have to come up with something else to do. Also, selling stuff online doesn't really generate much income, or at least for me it doesn't, and though I like it, I don't need it.

Now one morning, thinking about and maybe praying a little bit about getting that first locker, I was strongly impressed to read 1 Tim. 6. We already looked at a couple of verses, but let's look at the next section.

"But those who desire to be rich fall into temptation, into a snare, into many senseless and harmful desires that plunge people into ruin and destruction. For the love of money is a root of all kinds of evils. It is through this craving that some have wandered away from the faith and pierced themselves with many pangs."

Well as anyone can see, this applies to all people, but when we start wanting more than we have, we need to be careful. Ask yourself, do you want to be rich, and what does being rich mean to you? If so, what are you willing to do to get it? Do you think you might be willing to compromise your Christian principles to get rich? Earlier we spent a few minutes speaking about gambling, and isn't that a compromising of our Christian principles? It is, and you know it, but it is a snare, a trap, a foolish and harmful desire designed to take from you, not enrich you. It could be some other get rich scheme, but scheme is the magic word. Not everyone that falls into these snares and evil lusts will be destroyed, but for the most part it plunges or drowns people into ruin in one form or another. It could be it isn't just the love of money, but what money can do or get for us. And, at the end of the day, we see that this is a root of all sorts of evil.

But when we start craving or hungering for wealth, some versions call this greediness, we are in danger from wandering away from the faith. There is an intensity implied in craving and hungering, much like an addict must have his drugs, which can only be covetousness, which is idolatry; you cannot serve God and mammon. But it is this craving that has caused many to wander away from the faith. The Apostle Paul gives us the example of Demas. In Colossians and Philemon, Paul mentions Demas in a positive light, but in 2 Timothy we read that Demas has "utterly abandoned" Paul, having loved this present world. One commentator wrote that this abandonment had "the idea of leaving someone in a dire situation." We have a warning and then a description of these people in 1 John 2:15. "Do not love the world or the things in the world. If anyone loves the world, the love of the Father is not in him." (ESV)

So are those people we see wandering from the faith really Christians? We all know Christians who have strayed for a while, and then repented, but again those words from 1 John tend to haunt us. "They went out from us, but they were not of us; for if they had been of us, they would have continued with us; but they went out that they might be manifest, that none of them were of us." None of us truly knows the heart of another, and we see Christians, including ourselves, that have at times done things which shouldn't be done, but at the end of the day if someone wanders from the faith and doesn't come back we have to wonder. Sometimes we want to say something dogmatically, but let us leave judgement to God.

But if you are a Christian who has wandered from the faith, you have pierced yourself with many sorrows. It is the image you get of a piece of meat being skewered so it can be roasted over an open fire. You have pierced your soul and whatever problems you are going through is probably a direct result of you wandering off. God will chastise His children in order to get them back on track and to repent. Others like those dead flies that spoil the apothecary, have so stunk up the name of Christianity, that they finish their days on earth separated from the people of God. They may or may not be Christians, but let's move on.

It could be that you don't crave more, or desire to be rich, and we will also assume you are not deceiving yourself. So what is it that you do want? Are you seeking significance or purpose in life, or just bored and need something to do? It could be some sort of combination of all these things, but as I read these words that day, the answer became clear as crystal.

"But as for you O man of God, flee these things."-ver.11

Now I know that the word of God speaks to all of us, and this verse is speaking to all Christians, whether it is a man, women, or child. We are to flee those things which might even tempt us, even if they are not necessarily sinful things in themselves. There are many things that we desire that can draw our focus and time away from Christ. We are to flee those things; for me it was to not attempt to get a locker. It doesn't always happen, but I asked a specific question and got a specific answer. Instead of getting a locker, I was to pursue something else, and that was righteousness, godliness, faith, love, steadfastness and gentleness. We read this in the last half of verse 11, and again, though this was my specific answer that day, this is something all Christians are to do at all times.

We are to flee the things of this world that tend to ungodliness. And our running away isn't aimless, but in a chasing after something else. Go ahead and finish reading verses 12-14. This is not simply a letter from Paul to Timothy, but the Word of God, from the Holy Spirit, to each one of us personally. He is charging us to fight the good fight of faith, to take hold of eternal life, and to keep the commandment unstained and free from reproach.

So are you doing that, living a life free from reproach? Often times our deeds of sin give an occasion to the enemies of the Lord to blaspheme, as we read in 2 Samuel 12 concerning David and his affair with Bathsheba. Romans 2:24 reminds us also that many times we are the cause for people to speak badly of God. We have said it before, but if we don't take our Christian life seriously, why should anyone take us seriously when we proclaim the gospel? First Peter 4:3 is a verse that comes to mind when the things of this world start creeping in. "We have spent enough of our past lifetime in doing the will of the gentiles." When we became new creations, born again by the Spirit of God, we were to put away all those things that the world craves after; have you?

We are not going to write it all out, but read Colossians 3:1-7 and take it to heart.

"If then you were raised with Christ, seek those things which are above, where Christ is, sitting at the right hand of God. Set your mind on things above, not on things on the earth. For you died, and your life is hidden with Christ in God."-v. 1-3

You were bought with a price, and you are not your own.-Shalom

JEREMIAH 13

There comes a point when God's people can go so far in sin that He gives them over to their own way. It isn't that they couldn't repent and be forgiven, but they will not repent because they love their sin too much. God is longsuffering and patient, and always gives ample time and warnings for repentance. But there comes a time when chastisement no longer works. In Isaiah 1:5 God asks His people why they should be stricken again. Chastisement hasn't been doing any good. We are going to be looking at Jer. 13, as if it is one of those last calls to repentance, but read chapter 14 when you get a chance. Read what the Lord says at the end of chapter 14.

"Do not pray for the welfare of this people. Though they fast, I will not hear their cry, and though they offer burnt offering and grain offering, I will not accept them. But I will consume them by the sword, by famine, and by pestilence." (ESV)

We could say a lot more on chapter 14, but it is 13 we want to concentrate on. Often times God uses parables to teach us, and we are reminded of all those Jesus used, but many times, especially in the Old Testament, God used visual parables to get people's attention. It also might be helpful to read chapter 13 or have a bible handy since we aren't going to go verse by verse, but will be skipping around a little bit.

Though these posts are written primarily for the Christian disciple, those of you who have not yet placed your faith in Christ can benefit too. Much, if not all that was written in this chapter was for a people who were for all intents and purposes not saved, but thought they were, so you will fit right in. But those of us who really are Christians need to look at our lives and see if there is some sin that we refuse to give up. If so, what we are going to be discussing will hopefully cause you to come to your senses and repent.

It would be helpful to know a little or a lot of the history going on around the time of Jeremiah, but suffice it to say that Judah was on its death bed. In fact it was during Jeremiah's lifetime that Judah went into captivity, an event that Isaiah had foretold nearly a hundred years earlier. This was all happening because of their sin, and as mentioned earlier, this seems to be one of those last chances of repentance.

Now God told Jeremiah to go out and buy a linen loincloth and to not get it wet and to wrap it around his waist. I've got to admit that it isn't totally clear to me exactly what the loincloth was for. Some say it was a sash, which doesn't make sense to me, and some say it was a girdle worn on the outside. In either of these cases people would have seen Jeremiah wearing this expensive piece of clothing every day and when he no longer wore it would have had questions. There are other types of loincloths, but personally I think it was something to cover and support his privates, which we would call our underwear. Since it was made out of linen, it would have been especially expensive in that time, not your typical Fruit-of the Loom.

In any case, Jeremiah is obedient to the command of the Lord. Then God tells him to go to the Euphrates (River) and to hide the loincloth in a hole or cleft in the rock. Again, Jeremiah is obedient and does as the Lord has said. Where on the Euphrates River he went we don't know, but regardless, it would have been a trip that took many days. For this reason there are those who would tell us that it must have been some other river close by, with a similar name. I wasn't there that day with Jeremiah, so I am just going to take it on faith that what the bible tells us is true, and he really took that long journey. After many days, and I assume Jeremiah has made it back home, the Lord tells him to go back to the Euphrates and dig up the loincloth he hid there. Well, once again Jeremiah is obedient and does what he is told. Just an aside here, but how often are we obedient to those commands of God which in our eyes don't make sense? First, go buy some underwear, expensive underwear, and then go bury it by a river. Never mind it might take you a couple of weeks to get there and a couple more to get back. Then to top it off, you have to go back and retrieve it. It kind of makes our refusal to go visit our neighbor seem kind of trivial doesn't it.

Anyway, Jeremiah goes and digs up the loincloth and finds that it has rotted; it has spoiled and become good for nothing. Again we have to admire Jeremiah and his obedience, because he almost certainly knew that it would be totally ruined when he unearthed it. And that is the whole point God is trying to get across. The people of Judah and Jerusalem were a treasured people to the Lord, and just as a loincloth clings to the waist of a man, so God had made them cling to Him. He wanted them to be His people, a name, a praise and a glory, but they wouldn't listen. So just as the loincloth that Jeremiah had buried was useless, God was going to spoil their pride. They had become an evil people, refused to listen to God, and were good for nothing.

When we read the next section of this chapter, it seems as if all hope for repentance is gone, but as we shall see when we go a little further, there is still a glimmer of reform, a possibility of repentance. But before that we need to look at our own lives, and I am specifically speaking to myself and others who call themselves Christians. God in Christ has drawn us close to Himself. He dwells in us, and we are His people. But is there some sin in your life that you refuse to get rid of? Sometimes we think our religious activities make us immune to the discipline of God, and we become proud of what we think we have accomplished, not realizing that it is God working through us. If we are not careful we can begin to think that we are indispensable, and that God needs us. Nothing could be further from the truth, but it is that kind of attitude that causes us to think that we can sin without impunity. We would never say that out loud, or even think it, but our actions do. It is also a warning in that if you have an unrepentant heart, there is a good chance you have an unregenerate heart as well. If you refuse to repent after acknowledging the truth of your sin, then you have no cause to call yourself a Christian. And just to be clear, we aren't talking about those who repent and then fall into sin again. We never attain perfection in this life, but hopefully we are getting more Christ like all the time.

If you read verses 15-16, it seems as if it is one last call to repent. Listen and be not proud for the Lord has spoken. "Give glory to the LORD your God before He brings darkness." It is almost night. Some of you have heard the gospel so many times that you could proclaim it better than a believer, yet in your pride you will not believe. And why will you not believe? It is because you love your sin, whatever that is, more than God. The natural man is at enmity with God, and you refuse to be reconciled to Him by faith in Christ. You have a supernatural hatred which is clear evidence that you are dead in trespasses and sin.

I want to speak to the believer here for a minute, because some of you have become so entrenched in some sin, that you are good for nothing. But it is not too late for repentance, and we are to take comfort in that promise found in 1 John 1:9. "If we confess our sins, He is faithful and just to forgive our sins, and to cleanse us from all unrighteousness." Listen and pay attention, and do not be proud.

"But if you will not listen, my soul will weep in secret for your pride; my eyes will weep bitterly and run down with tears." (ESV)
There are some who would say that this is Jeremiah speaking of the anguish he would go through if these people did not repent. But this is the word of God and it is God that will weep in secret for their pride and it is His eyes that will weep bitterly and run down with tears. He will do this because the LORD's flock has been taken captive.

We always need to be careful in handling the word of God that we don't take things out of context or allegorize it to fit an agenda. Nevertheless, sometimes we can take a historical context such as we see here, and ask, does my life look like that? Have I been caught up in a sin for so long that I am no longer useful to the kingdom of God? We are talking to Christians here, ones who will not lose their salvation, but have lost their effectiveness because sin has taken them captive. We may have quenched and grieved the Holy Spirit to such an extent that He weeps bitter tears for us. Human emotions are the only way we can describe the grief and heartache we might cause to God, but I would imagine that it goes much beyond that. Believers do not have the mental capacity or language to describe what grief we cause God when we stubbornly and pridefully refuse to leave our sin. Enough on that for now.

God will chastise His children whether or not they understand and repent. Sometimes bad things happen in life to Christian people because of sin in the world, not because God is chastising them. But if you are living in known sin and bad things happen to you are you going to question God and ask why? It could be like it says in verse 22; it is because of the greatness of your iniquity. Look down at ver. 25 and see what else the LORD has said. "This is your lot, the portion I have measured out to you, declares the LORD, because you have forgotten me and trusted in lies."

How close have some of us come to that edge where God gives us up to our own ways? Is it even possible for a believer to reach that place where repentance is not available? It may be that a believer never repents of something in this life and holds on to that sin until they die, but I have to believe that God is always there pleading for us to do so. Yet, as we have read, if you forget the Lord and start trusting in lies and continue in your iniquity, do not be surprised or rather expect that life is going to throw you some difficulties.

If we had time in these posts, and I suppose we could drag it out, it had been better to spend a lot of time on this chapter, for there is much here concerning unbelievers as well as believers and we could all profit from it. Today is a good day for repentance. Think on these things as they might apply to you, and until we meet next, Shalom.

POINT OF NO RETURN

One of the difficulties in writing some of these posts is that the majority of the audience is unaware of some of the history behind the references given. Such will be the case today. However, the main point is that there is a line in the sand which individually or nationally, if crossed there is no turning back. Whether that is the case here in America or not, you be the judge, or actually God will be the judge, I am just going to throw a little history at you. This is just part of a much larger discourse, but sized down somewhat for FB.

"Then the Lord said to me, Even if Moses and Samuel stood before Me, My mind would not be favorable toward this people. Cast them out of My sight, and let them go forth. And it shall be, if they say to you, 'Where should we go?' then you shall tell them, 'thus says the Lord': Such as are for death, to death; And such as are for the sword, to the sword; and such as are for the famine, to the famine; And such as are for the captivity, to the captivity. And I will appoint over them four forms of destruction, says the Lord: the sword to slay, the dogs to drag, the birds of the heavens and the beasts of the earth to devour and destroy. I will hand them over to trouble, to all kingdoms of the earth, because of Manasseh the son of Hezekiah, king of Judah, for what he did in Jerusalem." Jeremiah 15:1-4

Three things we are going to briefly look at are 1. The inevitability of the event. 2. What the event is going to be. 3. The reason for the event.

1. Now it would be helpful to read chapter 14 also, but God's people the Israelites had continuously disobeyed his commands and precepts, and idolatry and insincere worship was rampant. Continually God sent prophets to warn them, but they for the most part ignored or scoffed at them. Judah, the southern kingdom had seen what had happened to the northern kingdom for their rebellion, yet refused to learn. And so, we reach this apex where God basically says there is no longer any hope. Even if such men as Moses and Samuel, men who in their day interceded on behalf of the people, even if they were to stand before God to intercede, he would not listen to them. We see a New Testament reference to this same idea, when in Romans 1, God finally gives people up to the consequences of their behavior and thinking. So there is no turning back, the people have crossed that proverbial line in the sand, but what is going to happen?

2. God is going to give the people up to death, the sword, famine and captivity. And in 586 B.C. Jerusalem was ransacked and the temple torn down, and much death and destruction attended all of this. And except for a small remnant which was allowed to stay, those who survived were taken into captivity. And why is this going to happen?

3. Because of Manasseh the son of Hezekiah, king of Judah, for what he did in Jerusalem. What little the bible says about Manasseh is primarily found in 2 Chronicles 33, and in 2 Kings 21. But he filled the land with idols and defiled the temple with idols and altars for the worship of false gods, and there was child sacrifice. It is written that he shed much innocent blood. When any nation takes upon itself the shedding of innocent blood, most specifically that of children, its demise is inevitable.

Now we can never forget that the people were complicit with the deeds of Manasseh, for they joined in his evil deeds. But as in most cases, the leader is just a reflection of the people's hearts. Righteous leaders tend to make things better, even if only temporarily, but evil leaders make things worse. The point being that the seeds of the nation's final destruction were planted long before the event.

America has been shedding innocent blood for a long time, and I am specifically relating this to abortion. Atrocities which have happened recently have been going on for a long time. But it seems as if many of our problems turned worse when the killing of the innocent was legalized. Or maybe it was when we elected an idol worshipper to lead us back in the 1960's. It could be just the total depravity of man coming to a head. One of these or something else or even none of the above, take your pick. It could be that you don't see all of these problems converging and getting worse and it just isn't here in America. We see it to a greater degree because we live here, but it is happening all over.

Now as stated before, this post isn't the full range of what was said concerning these few verses, but it is here to make you ponder the days we live in. Has America gone past the point of no return? Has the world gone past the point of no return? Have you gone past the point of no return in your own life? At some point in time there is going to be a judgement; it is inevitable. At some point in time the wrath of God will be unleashed against all unrighteousness. You personally will be held accountable for sin unless you repent or turn back to God, and accept the forgiveness that is to be had by faith in Jesus Christ, and the work that He accomplished through his life, death and resurrection. Even this is the gift of God, for the dead heart cannot make itself alive. Christ died to save his people from their sin; if you will not believe than apparently you are not one of his people. But, if you will not believe, it is because you choose not to, and the responsibility lies at your feet, for he calls to all. Yet it seems that only his people really hear his voice, for they are the ones who hear and believe.

Having said all this, now is the time to repent and believe. You never know what a day might bring, and tomorrow might be too late. And as long as there is breath in your lungs it is never too late to repent, no matter how bad you seem in your own eyes. But go and read of the repentance of Manasseh in 2 chronicles 33. If there is repentance for such as him, repentance is available for you. But, you must repent, I can't do it for you and neither can anyone else. However, if you refuse to listen, or believe and think it is just a bunch of fairy tales, and scoff at the idea of a God, just remember that you have been warned. So I leave you with this last little bit to ponder over.

"And the Lord God of their fathers sent warnings to them by his messengers, rising up early and sending them, because he had compassion on his people, and on his dwelling places. But, they mocked the messengers of God, despised his words and scoffed at his prophets, until the wrath of the Lord arose against his people till there was no remedy."-2 Chronicles 36:15-16

O HELL NO!

Over the years, whether it was on a website, a blog, or FB, or even in those few e-mails we sent, we knew there would be a number of people reading these posts who would never come to faith in Christ; this is for you.

Years ago there was a movie or a television show, I really can't remember because I only saw the last few minutes of it, but I never forgot it. And you were in the starring role. I may have some of the details wrong because it was so long ago, but you were riding in a train at night when a man named Mori came into the boxcar and sat down in the seat across from you. It was one of those darkest of nights, and the window shades were down, and if you had of raised the shade, the reflection of your face would be all that you could see. For a long time you both sat in silence until you couldn't stand it any longer and asked him his name and where he was headed. He replied that his name was Mori and he was delivering a package for his boss. Mori then called you by name and asked where you were headed. It caught you off guard because you were sure that you hadn't identified yourself, but you spouted off some destination, Salem I think it was, at which point he informed you that the train didn't go through Salem.

Thinking back, you tried to remember the station where you boarded, but even that was fuzzy. It seemed as if you had been riding the train for quite some time, but Mori was the only one you could recall having actually met. Opening the door of your riding car, hoping to see a porter or a fellow passenger in order to further inquire as to your whereabouts, you were shocked to see that it was as dark in the hallway as it was outside. Mori kind of smiled, if you can call it that, but it wasn't an evil smile or a smirk, but it was the smile of someone who has you trapped, you just don't know it yet. There was a little more chit chat, all of it disconcerting since Mori seemed to know all about you, but finally he informed you that the train was arriving at your destination. Protesting that if the train didn't go to Salem, it couldn't be your stop didn't seem to faze Mori in the least, in fact he started laughing. He had turned away from you to put on his overcoat and hat which he had taken off earlier and turning back around you saw him for what he truly was. Peering at you was a skull, laughing hideously, and he began dragging you off the train screaming, and the last words you remember him saying before he vanished, was "welcome to hell."

Time passes a little different down here, and whether that night was ten years ago or ten decades ago is hard to determine, but your words that night are as clear today as they were then, and that is "O hell no." In fact they are the same words or something like that anyway that all those entering the gates of hell say. And the words above the gate which said abandon hope all ye who enter here is seared in your mind and becomes a greater reality every day.

How many centuries have you been down here now, six or seven maybe? You vaguely remember how many years you lived before you died and came to this place, but it wasn't very long was it. Fifty or sixty you said once, but with the continuous torment of fire and pain and anguish the memory is slowly fading. That isn't the worst of it you would say, but the torment is such that we have no human words to describe it. There is the blackness of darkness, because the fire burns with no light. Also, though it is a darkness which can be felt, there is a sense of sight. There is isolation while at the same time knowing those who are with us. We see those who we influenced and damned to this place by our behavior, and we see those who did the same to us. The torment and torture we inflict upon one another is indescribable, but that is nothing compared to what we endure because of the wrath of God.

It's been at least twenty millennia now, and nothing has changed has it? There was a brief moment, how long it lasted you don't remember, but you stood before the judgement seat of Christ. Everyone received a new body. It was really the same body we had before we died, but it was new in that it was different. No longer was it susceptible to corruption, but it was the perfect body. Being indestructible meant that the torments you felt before were just increased because now you felt them also through the body. But there is another torment which sometimes surpasses the physical, though in reality it is all continuous, and that is the memory of that day; it is seared in your mind.

The beauty and peace and love of the place was overwhelming, and the light was just so beautiful it was beyond description. You didn't actually feel it, but you could tell, and when you came before Jesus it was indescribable. All you could do is fall on your knees and worship and cry out with the rest of creation, Jesus is LORD. But you knew, even before it was said, that you would be returning to hell, and the memory of that day is as tormenting as the fire that burns; it is seared in your mind.

It was Jesus, and while the memory of everything else is slowly fading, the sight of Jesus is as vivid now though ages have passed, as it was on that day of judgement. The perfection of His being was such that even now words can't begin to describe it, and when He looked at you and said "I never knew you", and had you set to the side along with all the others that He didn't know, you began to weep. You weren't the only one, and many began to start cursing and blaspheming and saying all kinds of hateful things against God, and to your astonishment the same types of things were spewing forth from your own mouth.

To your right you saw a group of preachers who had spent a lifetime telling their congregations the way of salvation, many of whom believed the gospel and were going to spend eternity with Jesus. Even now you remember their cries and pleas, "Lord, Lord, did we not prophesy in your name, and cast out demons in your name, and do mighty works in your name?" But Jesus looked at them and said depart from me, I never knew you. Then looking around, Jesus said those words which he said while living upon the earth, "Not everyone who says Lord, Lord, will enter the kingdom of heaven, but the one who does the will of my Father who is in heaven."

At your left you saw a bunch of people that numbered in the thousands if not millions, who were in shock. You thought you recognized a few of them from hell, and knew they were returning there just like you. But they kept saying there must be some kind of mistake. Most of them had attended church many years, singing in the choir, helping teach Sunday schools, been baptized, and if the church doors were open, they were there. It shocked you too, but then you remembered what someone told you once, and that is some people do a lot of stuff thinking that God will then owe them something. But it is faith in what God does for us that counts. You remembered that little girl who was a friend of your daughter who came over one day and recited what she had learned in Sunday school a couple of days before. You remember how she said it too. "John 3:16. For God so loved the world that He gave His only begotten Son, that whosoever should believe in Him would not perish, but have eternal life. John 3:16"

Your daughter became a Christian not long after that, and you remember many times that her and her friend would often tell you about Jesus and salvation, but you just weren't interested. There was more important stuff to do. Sunday was the day you liked to go golfing with your buddies and in the fall and winter, football and then basketball was in season, and you couldn't miss that. It wasn't that you were a bad guy, in fact sometimes you would donate to charity, and give money to the guy on the street corner. You took care of your family, didn't cheat on your wife, paid your taxes, and overall were a pretty outstanding member of society.

Looking around, you saw that yours was the biggest group. There was a lot of murmuring that we haven't done anything wrong, why are we being punished? Now everyone admitted that they weren't perfect, never stopping to think that it is perfection that God requires, and again you remembered what your daughter had said on more than one occasion. Because Jesus was perfect and without sin, and died in our place, all our sin being placed on Him, by faith, we believe that His dying in our place and living a perfect life of obedience will be accredited to us, so that when God looks at us, He sees perfection. Not our perfection, but Jesus' given to us. It sounded like a bunch of nonsense to you then, but now it is too late. Those words which you heard, that it is appointed once for a man to die, but after that the judgement, is clear as crystal.

Sometimes you remember that day. It has been millennia of ages now, and the stench of your burning flesh is as repulsive now as it has ever been and the pain just as great. If it was just a match burning your finger you could stand it for a minute, maybe even sticking your hand on a hot burner for a few minutes could be withstood, but this is fire and brimstone which never ends, and never ceases to cause pain. You are now as great a blasphemer against the name of God as any, and at the same time know that it is sin which placed you here and keeps you here. There is no comfort in knowing that you deserve to spend eternity in hell, and it is further aggravated by knowing you will spend eternity in hell.

We close by letting the reader know that though you have endured torment, torture and pain of anguish that goes beyond description, it has not ended. What is longer then millennia of ages? Perhaps we could say ages upon ages, but that is too short; it is eternity. Now we will close with those two things which are constantly in your thoughts as you endure this eternity of torment, and that is Jesus is LORD, and abandon all hope ye who enter here.

"There is no peace for the wicked"-God